LEADING A THRIVING MINISTRY

Ten Indispensable Leadership Skills

Gil Stieglitz

ISBN: 978-0-9831958-4-9
Christian Living/Theology

Published by Principles to Live By
www.ptlb.com

Cover Design by John Chase

DEDICATION

*This book is dedicated to two men
who are shining examples of the leadership that this book
is all about. When I am in need of a living picture of what
a godly leader would do, I just look at these men.*

Norman Franklin Stieglitz Jr.
*Words cannot express the debt that I owe this man who
I call Father. His example, his wisdom, his generosity,
and leadership are a near perfect expression of what
the New Testament describes as a godly leader.*

Dr. Conrad Lowe
*God has on a number of occasions miraculously sent this godly
leader into my life to instruct, encourage, listen, and direct me.
I have benefited immeasurably from exposure to his leadership.*

TABLE OF CONTENTS

PREFACE

No book would be produced without the many people behind the scenes that make it happen. First, let me thank my incredible wife, Dana, and my three lovely daughters, Jenessa, Abbey, and Grace, who have allowed me to spend endless hours working on this book. They share my goal to help other families obtain all the blessings that God has for them. I also thank Sandy Johnson, my Administrative Assistant at Principles to Live By, and Dalene Lequieu, my Office Manager with the Western District of the E.F.C.A. They have allowed me to remain sane while working with these two wonderful non-profit organizations. Thank you, Scott Davis and the executive team at Adventure Christian Church for providing valuable suggestions on the raw manuscript. To the folks at Thriving Churches International, Inc., thank you for working alongside me to print this important resource. Last, but not least, let me thank the churches, organizations, and leaders I have worked with in their moments of need for the last thirty years. The wonder of leadership demonstrated and growing is amazing. There is a joy in ministry leadership that is unmatched in any other kind of endeavor. Lives are being changed and the Kingdom of God is advancing. Thank you for allowing me to focus you on a few skills to thrust your leadership forward.

Introduction: My Journey into Leadership

When I graduated from seminary I was ready to change the world. I was convinced that God was waiting for me to graduate so His worldwide program could begin in earnest. God in His infinite wisdom put me out on the back side of the desert where I could do little damage. The church that called me as their senior pastor was a little church plant in the southern Mojave Desert of California. I was their first full time pastor. There were fifty people in the church and six hundred fifty houses in the town. The church met in an abandoned sales trailer. The town was isolated and forty-five minutes from the nearest city with typical services. God had isolated me. I was excited about ministry and plunged into ministry to everyone in the town. Our church was the only church of any kind meeting in this community. It was an exciting time of connecting people to God, fixing marriages, helping the bereaved, and being "Pastor" to a whole town. On Easter Sunday two years later we had two hundred eighty people at worship services. I was convinced we were on our way to changing the world. It was wonderful. I thought that we would just keep on growing until almost everyone in town would go to my church.

Right after Easter a large group of people in the church began to hold meetings, express growing concerns about the future of the church, and openly discuss how to remove me as pastor. The disgruntled minority came up with ten to fifteen major issues which demanded my removal as the pastor. They pushed their complaints to force a congregational showdown. The result of the meeting was that we had a church split. We went from averaging two hundred at Sunday services to having about eighty people come to services on Sundays.

After spending most of the summer in the futile attempt of re-engaging the disaffected, I told the board it was time to start reaching out to new people. Two years later at Easter we were again over two-hundred people. It was a wonderful time of celebration and encouragement. Unfortunately, in the weeks after that service a whole new group of people began to leave the church and to have doubts about my abilities as a pastor. We had another church split. Our church was back down to eighty people.

For the second time I told the leadership board of our church that we needed to focus on reaching new folks with the gospel. And in about two years we were back up around two-hundred people again. And then the same thing happened again with different people and different issues. On four separate occasions our church grew to about two-hundred people and then blew up and went back down to about eighty. I did not have a clue how to stop it from happening.

When it was getting ready to take place the fifth time, the lead elder of our church pulled me aside after a mid-week meeting. He let me know that the board had met (without my being invited) and they wanted to assure me that they thought I was a wonderful pastor, but it was clear that I didn't have a clue what I was doing. They were tired of losing their friends. This every-two-year explosion needed to stop. The board agreed that something needed to be done, so they had approved the money and the time off for me to attend a class that would tell me how to fix this problem the church was having.

I asked him what seminar I should attend. He replied that he did not know what it was. I was going to have to find it, attend it, learn, and report back to the board. I will forever be grateful to this group of godly leaders who gave me room to grow and believed that our church's problems could be fixed. I knew how to pastor, but I did not know how to lead a church to God-honoring healthy growth.

Sitting in my office the next few days I did not know what to do. A flyer came across my desk for a "Breaking the 200 Barrier Seminar." It sounded like the problem that our church was having. I signed up for the seminar and invited a pastor friend of mine to come along. I sat on the front row and took copious notes as John Maxwell, Conrad Lowe, and Peter Wagner explained things about the church that I had never heard before. They talked about leadership, prayer, evangelism, organization, and church issues from a different point of view. For three days I drank in new information. I reported to the church board that there were six specific things that our church needed to do differently to keep from blowing up.

I implemented those six changes, and we began to see growth. We were at about one hundred seventy at the time and everyone was expecting the next blow-up to happen at the coming Easter. But we grew through two hundred and then two-hundred fifty and problems. We kept implementing and learning, and we grew through three hundred and then three-hundred fifty. The board sent me to another seminar -- "Breaking the 400 Barrier" -- and we grew to four hundred and then four-hundred fifty. We kept growing past five hundred and past six hundred and then eventually past seven hundred. We never had the problems that had plagued us so many times. We had other challenges, but we did not split. We never blew up ever again. I began to learn to lead. If the church is going to make the difference it should, Christian leaders must begin to lead and not just to minister.

The Definition of Leadership

A working definition of leadership is ***causing action in the right direction***. This definition recognizes that all kinds of people lead in small, large, and even unintended ways. Some people only do this leadership function occasionally, while other people do it every day. Some lead ten people and some lead millions. The more consistently other people look for you to "cause action in the right direction," the higher level leader you are. Therefore the leader must know how to cause the action to happen and what is the right direction.

What is the ultimate right direction for leaders in church work? This is easy. God has aimed the church at accomplishing five essential things:

Evangelism   (Matthew 4:19)
Discipleship   (Matthew 28:18-20)
Worship   (Matthew 4:10)
Compassion   (Matthew 5:45-48)
Fellowship   (John 13:34,35)

Everything that a church does should be about accomplishing one of these purposes that God gave the church. When it is all said and done and we stand before Jesus, leadership in the church will come down to: Did more people come to faith in Jesus because of your leadership? Did more people live out the full Christian life because of your leadership? Did more people have authentic worship experiences with God because of your leadership? Did more people become transparent with their fellow Christians and with God because of your leadership? Did more people serve the Lord and the afflicted, poor, oppressed, and needy because of your leadership?

Causing action in the right direction is largely a set of skills that leaders can learn and master. Non-leaders will find this set of skills almost impossible to master. But leaders can grow in their leadership. In much the same way that basketball players can develop in their ability to execute the skills of playing basketball - dribble the ball, pass the ball, shoot the ball, and rebound the ball - so leaders can learn the skills of leadership. Yes, some people will be able to execute one or more of the skills with greater ability. If the kingdom of God is to advance, many more leaders must learn how to lead at higher levels. Remember that Moses recognized there were leaders of ten, leaders of fifty, leaders of one hundred, and leaders of one thousand (Exodus 18:25). In other words, there were people who could effectively lead ten people but not fifty people. There were people who could effectively lead fifty people but not one hundred people. There were people who could lead one hundred people but not one thousand people. If God has given us leadership ability, then we should maximize that ability and lead for God's glory. One of the tragedies is that men and women who have abilities to lead at the next level have not honed the crucial leadership skill(s) to allow them to reach their full potential of leadership gifting.

It is helpful to divide leadership into ten basic skills. I realize that there are more than ten skills in leadership, but I have found that these ten are so basic that they provide a foundation for every ministry. How leaders do at these skills determine the level of that ministry. The ten essential leadership skills are the ability to:

- **Conceive and Communicate Vision**
- **Define Reality Clearly**
- **Recruit Next-Level People**
- **Develop Leaders**
- **Initiate and Manage Change**
- **Use People skills**
- **Make Wise Decisions**
- **Systematize and Delegate**
- **Raise and Manage Resources for the Vision**
- **Self-Discipline**

We are talking about the skills of leadership not gifting for leadership. Skills can be learned; gifting and aptitude cannot. It is a tragic waste to have gifts and aptitudes and not to develop those for full kingdom impact. It is the skills detailed in this book that allow maximum leadership. Leaders are to develop themselves with all diligence in their leadership ability (Romans 12:8). Some leaders may not have a high in leadership gifting; but through hard work, their effectiveness will rise sometimes beyond those with high aptitude but little diligence. It is obviously best when high aptitude is married to high skill.

Jesus goes out of His way to say that the kind of leadership that He is advocating will be a different form of leadership than the "everybody do it my way" form of leadership (Mark 9:35). He wants servant leaders. He wants leaders who achieve righteous objectives with followers still vibrant and healthy. These have been called Godly Leaders, Servant Leaders, High Integrity L eaders. They really care about the people they lead. They look at the ethics, consequences, and wisdom of their decisions not just if it works for them. Let's do a deep dive into the essential skills of leadership.

HOW TO USE THIS BOOK

This book was written so that Christian leaders would begin doing real biblical projects that would empower them to be better leaders. Therefore if the exercises are not attempted, this book will be of little value to you. The genius of this book (if there is any) is not what I write but what you will do through the exercises at the end of each chapter.

Personal Study

This book can be a personal study. If you are working through this book alone, then take each chapter and do at least one of the projects in that chapter. Mark any exercises that are especially helpful. If you find that one exercise is particularly helpful, then stay with that one exercise for a month or longer. In fact, that effective exercise may become the backbone of your winning strategy. If you want to add others to this one that are particularly powerful, then keep going through the book and adding more. But it is more important that you discover how to lead than that you finish the book in a certain time frame. Keep doing new exercises until you have gone through the material at least once. You should be in a different place at the end of that cycle. You may then want to get into a group study in which you go through the material with others.

Mentor-Directed Study

This book can be done as a mentor-directed study. This is where a well respected, godly leader takes you through this material and evaluates your progress. Each week or month the mentor will assign chapters and exercises. The next time you gather together, significant amounts of time should be given to describing what happened when you did the exercises. If nothing was done then the same exercises should be repeated. It is crucial to not be in a hurry to get through this material. It is far more important that the material make lasting change and impact. In my opinion the mentor-directed study is the most powerful and effective way of deploying this type of soul stretching material. One of the most effective ways I have seen a mentor-directed study get started is for the person with the desire for a mentor ask a person that they highly respect to mentor them over this material. The mentor is asked if they would be willing to meet with the individual or small group and walk them through the material.

A second way that a mentor-directed study can be initiated is by the mentor. He/she can pray and ask the Lord to direct them to those who might be ready for a study like this one. Ask people God has put on your heart if they would be interested in growing deeper through a weekly study of this type. If they say yes, then sign them up and put them in a small group. If they say no, that is okay, they are just not ready.

Class or Lecture Series

This book can be covered as a Bible Study Class or Adult Sunday School Class. If there are less than six people in the class, I would recommend that you adopt the Mentor format rather than the Class style. But if there are seven or more, then the lecture style can work quite well. This study – or one like it – should be a constantly repeating part of leadership development in every church. The best class format divides an hour and a half into three approximately equal segments of about thirty minutes. Start with prayer and about twenty to thirty minutes of sharing in small groups of three to four people about how the exercises went from the last week. If there is wide spread misunderstanding on the exercises that were taught the last time, then they should be explained again and assigned again. Then there should be a twenty to thirty minute lecture on the next set of exercises. Sometimes the information and/or exercises are so crucial that complete focus must be on a very limited amount of material. Remember that the goal is not to have people impressed with the teacher. The goal is to build godly leaders. This will only take place if they are actually doing the exercises. Finally, the last twenty to thirty minutes should be set aside for actually doing the exercise in class. Have the people in the class actually try out the exercises. Then have the class commit to doing particular exercises during the week.

Because the church is always in need of more godly leaders, I would strongly suggest that the material in this book or material like this be set up to be a constantly running class or support group in every church. Remember the goal is demonstrated skill in leading. If a project or exercise needs to be repeated, then repeat it.

LEADERSHIP SKILL # 1 – CREATE AND COMMUNICATE A COMPELLING VISION

There is a world of difference between doing ministry and leading ministry. I was very good at doing ministry but was largely clueless about leading ministry. One of the most significant steps that I took into leading ministry was the chart you see below.

Ministry Vision

One of these charts should be filled out for each lifestage ministry of the church.

Worship Matthew 4:10	Evangelism Matthew 4:19	Fellowship John 13:34, 35	Discipleship Matthew 28:18-20	Service / Compassion Matthew 5:45-48

I began meeting with the leaders of ministry in our church to discuss this chart. In our church were the children's ministry, the youth ministry, the adult ministry, the men's ministry, the women's ministry, and the music ministry. All of these ministries were led by lay volunteers when I started. I met with each leader and their teams separately. After prayer, I began by reminding them that the church is only supposed to do five things: Worship, Evangelism, Fellowship, Discipleship, Service/Compassion. If we do these five things, then we will be fulfilling Christ's purpose for the church. Our job is not to do dinners or programs or even sing; these are just ways to accomplish the five purposes. This usually helped them realize the difference between a strategy and the purpose for that strategy.

Then I would ask them how they wanted to accomplish the purposes of the church in their ministry in the next six months. What followed was a wide ranging discussion and brainstorming session about how a specific ministry could accomplish Christ's purposes. This was always energizing and stretching. Sometimes people needed to be reminded about the definition of one of the purposes. Sometimes the leader(s) could not think of any ways to accomplish that purpose in their ministry. Many times I would ask them to pray, think, and talk about this with their whole team and get back with me in two to three weeks. Occasionally I would throw out ideas for a particular purpose if the group was stuck or needed to think in new directions. But I was not trying to decide for them.

I would also ask them how many people they thought their ministry could reach, impact, attract, or engage in the various categories. I asked them to pray before they gave me a number. What was God saying to them? What was His stretch goal?

It was not until later that I realized that this chart and these discussions were the second part of a system for constructing a vision for a ministry. The two most exciting things about this chart were, first, that it focused a specific ministry on Christ's purposes and not the programs and events of that ministry. Amazing amounts of energy are released when people grasp why they are doing all the programs. The second crucial thing about this chart is that I was leading people to do ministry instead of doing it all myself. I was no longer the bottleneck on how much ministry could be done. As soon as people understand what ministry is, they will be energized to invent all kinds of new ways to make it happen. Then your job as pastor is to try and direct all that energy instead of supplying it.

As I came to realize later, the above chart was the second step in what became a four-month process each year of constructing a vision that energized and released the church to invade our community for Christ. If you get the vision right and communicate it passionately, it will energize the congregation. In a larger church the process may take longer and may seek to envision life for the next thirty-six months.

Constructing a Vision for Ministry

Each year it would take four months to conceive, construct, and begin communicating a compelling vision for the coming year of our church's life. For me it began in August. The vision began as a month of long walks with God in 115 degree heat in the Mojave Desert. I would cry out to God, "What is your vision for this church?" "What do You want to do in and through this church next year?" "If you had free reign in this church, what would you do in Worship, Evangelism, Discipleship, Fellowship, Compassion, Children's, Youth, Adults, Men's, Women's, Facilities, and Finances?" I would walk through the streets of our town, out in the desert, and all over the church property with a pad of paper and those categories across the top or down the side of the paper. Whenever I had an idea, I would write it down. I wrote down hundreds of ideas. At first I did not evaluate or filter the ideas; I just wrote them down as they came to me. I assumed that some of them came from me and some of them came from God, but I did not know which were which yet. As the month of prayer progressed, certain ideas kept coming back and having more resonance and power, while others just seemed off somehow. I would write and rewrite the list until it was more focused and less scattered. But I purposely did not try and "finish" it as I learned that it had a number of additions and revisions that were coming. At this point it was just what I thought God was saying. Other leaders would need to pray and weigh in before we had the vision from God for the coming year.

If God had free reign in this church (unlimited money – unlimited help – no pettiness), what would He want us to do or try in each of the following areas?

Evangelism
Discipleship
Worship
Fellowship
Compassion
Music/Celebration Arts
Children's: W E F D S/C
Youth: W E F D S/C
Adults: W E F D S/C

Facilities
Finances

The second month is a month dedicated to helping the top leaders to go through a similar process of praying, writing, evaluating, adding, and subtracting in their specific areas. In a smaller church this top level is the board. In a larger church this is the top level of staff with potentially some board input. I would often ask the top leaders in the church to answer the same question in prayer that I had grappled with for the previous month. "If God had free reign in this church what would He do in Worship, Evangelism, Fellowship, Discipleship, Compassion, Children's, Youth, Adults, Men's, Women's, Facilities, Finances?" I was often amazed that what they wrote dovetailed with what I sensed from God. I was also very encouraged when they added new insightful ideas. When our church was small, I would collect the board's answers on paper without sharing what they wrote with the whole group until I had the ability to sift through it and combine it with what I had prayed through. Then I would reintroduce what I garnered in prayer and what they wrote as a unified whole that we could pray about over the next month. Remember, the constant focus is on the five purposes of the church, not a favorite program or pet project. The month was spent praying and talking until we could all support what was written down as the vision. Sometimes some of them suggested programs from their past church experience which were out of place. We learned to ignore those most of the time.

The third month is spent praying with and communicating with the next level of leadership in the church. There is still room for input and some changes, but the main thing at this second level is that they sense that they hear about the vision and goals before the congregation does. There must be a special effort to communicate with second-level leaders and key influencers as they must buy into the vision of the church. This is also the month that the vision is matched up with the budget. If the resources and budget are not connected to the vision, then everyone knows that the vision is not a serious proposal. It takes money to do ministry and if you are going to do one strategy, it will take away money from another strategy. I must admit this "third month" took two months many times because of meetings involved in creating the budget.

The fourth month is when the vision is communicated to everyone in as many ways as possible. It is communicated in letters, prayer requests, budget line items, sermons, banners, posters, emails, website notices, and personal conversations. Communicating the vision for our church started with the printed budget proposal for the next year. We asked people to look at the budget and pray about it before the congregational vote. Our congregation had to actually be presented with the opportunity to say that, yes, they too sensed that this was where God wanted us to go in this next year. But this worked to our advantage as a communication tool.

During this fourth month (November for our church), I would preach a whole sermon on the vision. The whole Sunday was dedicated to where we were going and where we had been in the last year. We would look back at the last year and read out what God had accomplished through the church so people could see what had been done.

"We saw three hundred people pray to receive Christ this last year!"
"Go ahead and stand up if you became a Christian in this last year."
"We had over sixty percent of our church involved in small groups."
"If you were involved in a small group this last year, then raise your hand and keep it up so everyone can see."
"We fed and clothed between five hundred and seven hundred people every month through our Compassion ministry."
"Stand up if you were a part of that amazing amount of love shown to people in need this last year."
"We saw over fifty new people become members this last year."
"Raise your hand if you became a member this last year."
"This last year we grew from five hundred to five hundred seventy-five at worship on Sunday."
"If you started coming in the last year to this church, thank you and wave your hand."

We went through each of the five purposes and talked openly about what had happened in the various ministries during the last year. We talked about children's ministry and what God had done through the wonderful people leading and volunteering in that ministry. We talked about student ministries and how God was working in that ministry. We talked about women's ministry and men's ministry. Too often the church does not celebrate what God has done. It was very encouraging for people to know that their church was focused on Christ's purposes and was keeping track of what was happening.

After exploring and celebrating what had happened last year, we then walked through the vision and where we thought God was leading us in the next year. Here is what we believe God wants to do through us this next year. We invited everyone to become a part of next year's vision. This sermon on vision and celebrating the last year was recorded and handed out to people who wanted to know what our church was about.

"We see this next year as a time to reach out and grow deep."
"We believe that God has only asked the church to do five things: Evangelism, Discipleship, Worship, Compassion, & Fellowship."
"We are trusting God that two hundred plus people will make professions of faith."
"We are expecting seventy-five plus people will be added to our worship services."
"We plan on welcoming fifty new members to the church."
"We are planning and preparing for four hundred people to be training how to be better Christians in our classes and small groups."
"We believe that God wants us to touch our community with Christ love by continuing our food and clothing ministry but also reaching into the schools with a mentoring mom program for teens who become pregnant."
"Let me tell you more about what God has laid on our hearts and how you can be a part."

Understanding the Vision Thing

A vision is a very powerful thing. It compels people to be involved. If it is done right, it will cause people to get involved or get away. If a leader doesn't have a vision, he doesn't know where he is going. It would be like a family leaving on a vacation without picking a destination. They would just be driving around. Unfortunately most churches do not know where they are going and are just driving around hoping God or someone will do something.

Every ministry must know where it is going and why it is doing the things that it is doing? Why should we work so hard? What are we trying to accomplish? This is the preferred future; the vision for where the church is going in the next twelve to thirty-six months. People need to know specifically what is important and what is not important in the next twelve to thirty-six months. The internal feeling -- when you are following a compelling vision -- is "If we do these things, then the future we want will come true." Every year the leadership of the church must construct and then communicate the vision of the church (very large churches do this every three to five years).

A ministry cannot simply do what it did last year and expect to be healthy and growing. Even if it does the same dinners, programs, events, and services, it must invest those activities with new meaning and new purpose. Churches and ministries stagnate and decline because there is no inspired plan for how to accomplish God's objectives in the coming year. Church is about doing God's will in the world. What does He want to accomplish in the coming year? What is He troubled about in our community? What does He want to fix, close, open, change, or rearrange? It is simply not responsible to suggest that by the sameness of our programs the Almighty God of the Universe wants to do nothing new or nothing different. The God who created the world is bursting with ideas, solutions, grace, mercy, and hope – a vision taps into Him and puts some specificity to it.

A vision for a ministry is answering one fundamental question. What does God want us to do in the major areas of ministry in the next year to accomplish His purposes? This means that lots of dreaming, praying, planning, discussing, and interacting must take place to gain clarity on God's vision for a church.

Constructing God's Vision and Communicating It?

Let's go back and look at those months of prayer, discussions, planning and communicating, and look at them from a little different angle.

Month #1: Pray for God's ideas, solutions, and direction

Doing church work is a spiritual enterprise and the ideas for the coming year must not be your invention; they must be the result of lots of prayer. This should be done three to four months in advance of when the vision is needed to be made public so the vision can be submitted to the various parts of the church for additions, deletions, suggestions, and upgrades. I recommend taking a month to pray and cry out to God about what He wants to do in His church in the coming year. I would usually ask myself one question to jumpstart the process. "If God had free reign in this congregation – unlimited money and unlimited manpower – what would He want to accomplish in this church within the next twelve to thirty-six months?" Too often the pastor, ministry leader, and/or church asks the wrong questions. "What did we do last year?" "Can we get better results than we did last year?"

If God had free reign in this church what would He want us to do or try in each of the following areas?

Evangelism	
Discipleship	
Worship	
Fellowship	
Service / Compassion	
Weekend Services	
Children's	
Youth	
Adults	
Facilities	
Finances	

I would fill multiple sheets of paper as I walked, prayed, thought, and reflected over the course of a month. This process was always encouraging and challenging. I would write down actual numeric goals as well as unspecific new ideas. Just because I prayed about it did not make it the will of God for our congregation. I would need to later see if other people were sensing the same things from the Lord and whether they would confirm my ideas. Too many pastors spend time in prayer and then assume that what they receive in their times of prayer is the received will of God which is not subject to further revision and correction. We are not Moses and do not receive things in stone from God. This is the place where you can write down any new ideas and/or new directions that seem to be coming from the Lord.

A few years ago I worked with a large church that was rapidly declining. The church had largely accomplished the vision the pastor had set down ten years before. The original vision was expansive and powerful. It required great sacrifice and accomplished huge things in their city. He felt that his original "plan for the future" was still not completed. Technically he was correct; there was still about ten percent of the original vision left to be completed. What he failed to realize was that the original vision no longer motivated people to work, give, or reach out. He had achieved ninety-plus percent of the original vision, and it was time to re-invent and re-cast the vision for the church. Only when new staff was brought in to help the pastor could he "see" a new vision and the decline reversed. Only when a compelling vision for two years into the future was communicated to the congregation did the church become active. There is no reason for people in the pew to band together and make the sacrifices that are necessary to conquer new heights of ministry unless there are goals powerful enough to demand that they get involved.

If you are in charge of a specific ministry within the overall church, then you need to ask, "What does God want my ministry to accomplish in Worship, Evangelism, Fellowship, Discipleship, and Service/Compassion?"

Month 2: Have meetings with top-level leaders and get their ideas and changes to the vision

I found it most helpful to ask the leaders of the church and the leaders of a particular ministry to start with a blank sheet of paper and the same basic question that I started with. Bathe these meetings in prayer while collecting ideas, input, and suggestions. I usually did not share my vision with them until they had prayed and began sharing. On many occasions it proved far more effective to blend their vision and my vision and see the wonderful symmetry. Letting the key leaders have a say in the vision development engages everyone.

It is usually better to collect ideas and input through a whole month. Letting people see the whole of the vision or great ideas can be squashed with flippant evaluation. Some ideas will have to be discarded or changed, but that will often become obvious when the whole is viewed.

It may take a whole month of meetings to have the various leadership groups hammer out the actual vision for the coming year. This month should include prayer, discussion, finances, implications, and significant changes to the initial vision. After all of this input and molding, then it is ready to roll out to the key influencers.

The key influencers are not technically leaders in the ministry, but their opinion counts tremendously and they need to be included in the initial roll-out of the vision. They need to be able to push back on the ideas or the process of sharing the vision with the congregation.

Who are the key leaders in this church or ministry who need to have input to the ideas, goals, and programs of this church's vision?

Who are the key influencers in this church or ministry who need to have the information early?

Before I learned to lead the ministry, we would grow and then blow up when we reached a little over two hundred. One of the reasons that it kept happening is how I would fix problems and launch new programs. The following was my dysfunctional system for thrusting the church forward and fixing problems. I would notice a problem and personally try and fix it, sometimes without communicating what I was doing to the board, key leaders, or the congregation. Sometimes this worked and sometimes my fixes caused a greater problem because the right people did not know that something was going to change ahead of time. I was constantly offending good people because the solutions seemed unplanned, arbitrary, or at least unknown until they appeared. I felt that people just needed to trust me to do what was right. Many times I would analyze a problem, conceive of a solution, and implement it without talking with anyone else. It was not until I took the extra time to ask what others saw as the problems and what they thought were the possible solutions that we eliminated this "communication" problem. When I consulted and informed others, the solutions were more effective and easily absorbed. In the early years I had a "see the problem - fix the problem" orientation to everything in the church. As the church grew larger it became increasingly important for the leaders, influencers, and congregation to all agree about the problems and their solution before any changes were made. In many cases a well constructed and communicated vision is the fix for a "communication" problem.

Month 2 - Key question: Does the vision engage the real problems and needs of the congregation and the community?

There are times when no matter how spiritual you are or how much you pray, you are still trapped in your cultural, ethnic, age-related and socio-economic ideas of church. Therefore you must prod your vision as it is being created with the real world. Will this vision really accomplish God's purposes as well as solve the problems of your congregation and your community?

In 1994, the town that I ministered in went through a devastating economic depression and over thirty percent were unemployed and eventually seventy-five percent of the people abandoned their homes and moved away. That is right; three out of every four houses were boarded up and vacant. We could just not keep doing suburban church the way that we had always done it when this happened. We had to start financial counseling at a whole new level. We started recovery support groups for all kinds of problems. We helped form a volunteer police force in our town. Our style of ministry changed to reflect what was happening in the community. We were still doing evangelism, discipleship, worship, fellowship, and compassion; but it looked very different.

Let me give you a few other examples. There are a number of churches in the inner cities of America that have had to start their own banks so that reasonable home and business loans are available to people in their neighborhoods. In some communities the collapse of after school programming has meant that performing arts must now come through the church and not the public school.

I remember talking to a pastor of a very wealthy church tell me that he would be happy to help the poor if there were any in his church. And he was right; there were no poor people in his church. However, the county where his church facilities were located was one of the poorest counties in California, but he couldn't see the need because they didn't come to his church.

Another bizarre disconnect from the real world was by a pastor who was describing what his vision was for the coming year. He told me that he really didn't want non-Christians attending his church. He was called to minister to Christians who wanted to grow deep in Christian doctrine. His vision for his church was an ever deepening group of believers who remained unstained by the world. It is little wonder why that church slowly declined and remained irrelevant to the city at large.

The vision for the church must make a difference in real people and in the real world. God is not interested in just "spiritual" things happening. He wants people transformed, marriages saved, abandoned people gaining hope, etc.

Month 3: Construct a rough draft vision

The pastor and senior leadership team need to weave all the various inputs and ideas into a coherent vision. Think and talk about this as a rough draft. This rough draft may feel like the final draft to the pastor and staff because they have been praying and thinking about this for two months or longer by this point. But it is important to remember that a number of people have not seen it or have not seen it in all of its pieces. Their first look at it will cause a whole new round of creative discussions. This is a good thing. If it can be improved, then it should be improved. While this is a rough draft it should not include ideas that do not fit with the philosophy of ministry and strategy of the church. It should be as close to the final draft as possible while everyone understands that this draft will change.

The rough draft may be in paragraph, diagram, or bullet form; but it needs to spell out specifically where the energies, resources, and time of the church will be directed in the next twelve to thirty-six months. I have included a potential rough draft vision for a church of five hundred in Appendix 2.

Month 3: Matching the vision to the resources

Everyone is usually willing to dream about new ideas; but when the resources to make those new ideas happen are put into the budget, the discussion gets much more serious. After the euphoria of getting agreement on the new vision, the hard work of matching the budget to these ideas takes place. You are only committed to what you give money to.

It will be clear that you cannot do everything when you match the actual budget numbers with what you are hoping to do; but in church work there is faith, miracles, and blessings.

Many of the various ideas that have been put into the vision for the church can be added to existing programs without disturbing anything. Other bolder and bigger programs will require that something stop happening so that the new thing can happen. It is imperative that the leaders of an individual ministry be given the largest possible control in how the new ideas are incorporated into the budget. They should know what monies they will receive and then should make wise decisions about how to use that money to accomplish the five purposes of the church.

When our children's ministry cut the Vacation Bible School summer program to spend the money on a different evangelistic program, it got a lot of other people's attention. But more little children heard the gospel and more made professions of faith. When the adult's ministry decided to move away from adult Sunday School to mid-week small groups in order to increase discipleship, this got a lot of people's notice. But it increased our participation in discipleship from twenty-five percent to sixty percent of the Sunday morning adult population.

Month 3: Write and rewrite the vision until it draws people to be a part of it

The vision should be a slogan, a theme, a few sentences, a few paragraphs, and a detailed document. Use evocative images, stories, and three-dimensional images of the future to bring the future into clear focus in the present. The essence of a vision is a snapshot of the future twelve months to thirty-six months from now. In this future, here is what is happening that is wonderful and exciting. The future must become real. The way you talk about the vision must create a three-dimensional image in people's heads about something that they care about. Some aspect of the vision must capture a person's attention or they will not participate. Therefore it is imperative that the vision be communicated with stories, facts, objects, videos, pictures, and testimonials – anything that will make the future live inside of people's minds. Work over the phrases, stories, and concepts of the vision until they connect with people each time you use them.

Month 4 - 12: Communicate the vision with the congregation over and over again in multiple ways and multiple venues

The vision of the church cannot be just stated once. It must be referred to constantly throughout the year. It must be repeated every month from the main stage. Every day is a new day to inform at least one more person. Reading the vision should make people want to sign up to work and give.

Communicating the vision means to constantly talk about it, but more than that it means create a three-dimensional picture of the future when this vision is completed and what that look like. People will rally to a future that is already real in their heads. They want to see that future come to pass. People will work, sacrifice, and give to make a compelling vision happen. This means to send it out in letters; refer to it in sermons; talk about it every day; show video's about it; tell stories about completing the vision; share testimonials; pray for the vision; make signs that display parts or all of the vision. Recruit people to the vision; take time in the service every month to remind people about where you are going; use the vision to recruit people to serve in the church. Letters to the congregation should spell out new aspects of the vision each quarter. Keeping the congregation informed about how much progress is being made will also foster a buy-in to the vision. The vision should be the surest and strongest way to draw people to engage in the life of the church.

A healthy leadership system
communicates the direction everywhere

If the church has clear direction but it is not communicated effectively, then the church will not move forward. I have seen lots of churches with vision who have great goals and great ideas about what God wants them to do, but they never pursue them. They never communicate them. They never engage the congregation in accomplishing the goals. This means that the people in the pew stay largely uninvolved with the ministry life and just watch the professionals do the ministry. If you think you are communicating the vision of God for your church and people are not getting involved, it means one of two things: one, you are not communicating the vision; or two, your vision is not compelling.

The church must hear the direction and vision from every possible source so that no one can miss the direction. It must be clear where this church is going in the next twelve to thirty-six months. Not everyone may like the things you are trying to do or the emphasis of the church, but it cannot be ambiguous. The direction must be communicated in terms that resonate with everyone in the congregation. Why are we headed in the direction that we are headed? What will the results be when we get there? What convinced the leadership that this was the direction to go in? What problems are we trying to fix by this direction?

Communicating the vision in its full version, its parts, and its slogan version is done in every way possible. Here are a few of the ways:

Sermons	Conversations
Stage announcements	Vision desserts
Recruiting appointments	Letters
Email signatures	Prayer campaigns
Bulletin announcements	Banners
Ministry announcements	Testimonials
Videos	Slogans
New member classes	Budget
Give aways: pens, magnets, etc.	Magazines
Signs	Emails
Congregational meetings	Blogs
Web page	Twitter
Facebook	Personal discussions
Staff and volunteer evaluations	Newsletters
Weekly evaluations	Word of mouth
Newspapers	Advertising
Yearly, monthly, quarterly reports	

Most good leaders have had the problem of talking about the vision so much that they are sick of talking about it. But that is precisely at the point that the vision may be gaining traction and clarity in the congregation. The leader must be willing to constantly spew out the vision. Accomplishing these goals and these ideas is the guiding light of the next year to three years of their existence. If your vision is not worthy of exhausting yourself to see it accomplished, then do not expect much traction with the rest of the church.

If I were to come to your church and ask you or any one of the members of your church what you are trying to accomplish in your children's ministry in the next twelve months, they should be able to tell me. Unfortunately many churches are just trying to take care of the kids while the pastor preaches. Your people should be able to say something like:

- Ô We are trying to see four children pray to receive Christ every week
- Ô Have forty percent of the children make an actual change in their life each week
- Ô Have a children's worship attendance of one hundred fifty children on Sunday morning
- Ô Have each child invite at least three other children to attend during the year
- Ô Open a puppet ministry for children, producing four different puppet stories each quarter

The same detail and specificity should be prayed about, planned for, and pursued in each of the departments of the church.

LEADERSHIP SKILL #2 - DEFINE REALITY CLEARLY

Take an honest look at your ministry

- Ô Your ministry is either growing or it is not.
- Ô The congregation knows where the church is going or it does not.
- Ô The ministry has people becoming Christians every week or it does not.
- Ô People's lives are being transformed by your ministry or they are not.
- Ô The church has visitors or it does not.
- Ô Visitors to the church keep coming back and become members or they do not.
- Ô The weekend services transport people into the presence of God or they don't.
- Ô The people who attend your church invite their friends to church or they don't.
- Ô The children's ministry at your church either excites children or it doesn't.
- Ô The student's ministry at your church is attractive to teens or it isn't.
- Ô The adult's ministry changes people's lives every week or it doesn't.
- Ô People change because of the sermons or they don't.

Many pastors and Christian leaders are afraid of reality or fail to truly see it. Let me take you into one all too familiar case. A discouraged Pastor Bryan called me to help him sort through a problem in his church. He was the pastor of Oak Harbor Church (the names and some details have been changed to protect the innocent) in a suburb of Seattle. The church had been at twelve hundred when he came two years before. Now the church was down to eight hundred and falling rapidly. I asked Pastor Bryan why the church was having problems and declining. He cited a particular group of disgruntled lay leaders in the church. They were opposed to him and were blocking everything he was trying to do. One of the men had been at the church for years and had made a number of other pastors miserable also.

Bryan also told me about the ineffective women's ministry and the closed and unfriendly nature of the adult Sunday school classes. When I asked him about the strengths of the church, he emphasized his preaching. He was doing a verse by verse exposition of Romans. The series had been going eighteen months, and he was almost done with chapter one. He was really going in depth. He had also started an evening Bible class that was going deep in systematic theology. The people loved it, he said. After I suggested a few ways to deal with the problems that he cited, he asked me if I could meet with the staff to help them see the real problems in the church.

I agreed to meet with the staff the next time I was in Seattle to see if I could help the church stop the decline and begin moving forward for the Lord Jesus. When I was introduced as the consultant brought by Pastor Bryan to get a handle on the problems at the church, the room went icy cold. Because of a scheduling conflict, the Senior Pastor was not at this meeting. I told the staff and a few elders that Pastor Bryan had let me know that there were some problems in the church, and he was hoping I could help the church grapple with the problem. No one was interested in talking about the problems at the church. Eventually I asked if I could just listen to their perspectives on what was holding the church back from its full potential. This might help the real problems become visible and fixable. Eventually they agreed to share their thoughts as long as it was done anonymously. I stood at the board and began writing down without comment their ideas about the problems in the church. What was wrong? Why was the church declining? What were they hearing? What were they noticing?

I stood at the board writing for an hour and a half. There were over sixty different problems, concerns, issues, and comments. I was somewhat shocked that none of the issues that the pastor had mentioned made the list. I even mentioned the people and the issues that the pastor had mentioned as possible concerns, and they did not agree that these were issues. The list did include boring sermons, speaking over people's heads, too much time in Romans, and a distant impersonal pastor. When the list was complete, the whole staff embraced the list as an overview of the problems in the church. I allowed them to look at the comments for a while and then I asked, "What is the common denominator of all these concerns?" No one said a thing until I wrote in huge letters over the top of all of the comments: BRYAN. Then they nodded their heads, yes!!! All the problems in the church were directly or indirectly related to Pastor Bryan.

The pastor thought his preaching was a strength of the church and everyone else saw his preaching as one of the major problems. This is a major reality issue. The chairman of the church board happened to be in that meeting and he asked me to do that same exercise with the church board a couple of days later. I declined but suggested that he could do it since he had seen me do it. I just stated that he should ask the same question and write things down without comment or argument. If the board, without coaching or influence, wrote the pastor's list then the pastor was right. If the board gave the same list as the staff, then the pastor was not living in reality about his leadership or ministry. A week or so later the chairman of the board called to say that the board virtually reproduced the staff's list.

The board then sat down with Pastor Bryan and began discussing these concerns and their potential fixes. He could not believe that his preaching and leadership style were a major cause of the church's decline. Months went by with the two sides arguing about what the real problems were. I remember saying to myself as I talked with Pastor Bryan, "YOU ARE IN DENIAL!!!" "And you will most likely lose your job over this."

Denial is a problem for alcoholics, drug addicts, married couples, parents, and, yes, even pastors and Christian leaders. In this case, it did cost Pastor Bryan his job and the church moved on with a different pastor who could agree with them about reality. The first skill of great leaders is that they get a firm grip on reality.

The clear biblical example of great leadership demanding reality is Nehemiah. He was jolted into leadership by the report of the reality back in his ethnic homeland, Jerusalem. He was not ready to launch into action until he had received numerous reports about the situation in Jerusalem (Nehemiah 1:2,3). There was no way that worship of God could become viable in that part of the world without a working city. The city could not become a fully functioning city without a wall. The people who had went back to rebuild the city had been there for ninety-two years by the time of Nehemiah. They were not making progress; they were growing increasingly despondent. Fear, depression, and inaction gripped God's remnant. When Nehemiah's first steps of leadership were rewarded with position and title from the king, he made sure that he had an even clearer picture of reality when he actually got to Jerusalem (Nehemiah 2:11-15). Before he tried to present the compelling vision to the people, he made a midnight inspection of the walls to see the actual reality of the wall. It was this secretive reconnaissance mission that allowed Nehemiah to strategize the rebuilding process. He faced reality and realized that he had to mobilize the whole town if they were going to complete the project.

They were going to also need to build it quickly or the marauding bands of enemies would surely disrupt them, if not destroy the work. Good leadership makes sure that they know what they are dealing with before launching new plans and initiatives. He accomplished in fifty-two days what was not completed in ninety-two years.

Leaders are committed to grappling with things the way they really are without the sugar coating. You must welcome feedback, even if it is bad. You can't fix what you are unwilling to admit is a problem. There are four arenas that a leader must gain reality concerning: the objectives; the strategies; the people and organization; and the resources. When you have a firm grip on what is really happening in those four areas, you have laid an effective foundation for good leadership.

Ô **First, the objectives**
- o What are we trying to accomplish?
- o Where are we trying to go?
- o Are we accomplishing our objectives?
- o How much progress toward the objectives are we accomplishing?

Ô **Second, the strategies and systems**
- o What strategies and/or systems are we using to accomplish the objectives?
- o Are they working?
- o Could they be improved?
- o Would something else achieve the objectives more effectively?

Ô **Third, the people**
- o Do we have the right people (leaders) to achieve the objective?
- o Are the people organized in the best way to achieve the objectives?
- o Do the people we have need training?

- o Where do we need to add people?
- o Where do we need to change people?

Ô **Fourth, the resources**
- o Do we have the resources to accomplish the objectives?
- o How many resources do we really have?
- o Are we using the resources wisely?
- o How many resources do we really need?
- o Are there ways to increase resources?

Almost every unhealthy or declining church has a reality gap. Churches can foster a reality gap by believing that spiritual things are so different they can't be measured or aimed at. Even spiritual things can be pursued and measured.

I realize that technically Reality should come before Vision, but most potential leaders wake up to the vision thing before they are really willing to face the reality of their ministry. Recently I was asked to come to help a church in trouble, I began asking reality questions on day one rather than vision questions. This really helps people get a grip on what is happening and not happening. My usual first steps is to weekly measure the actual numbers of what is happening in Evangelism, Discipleship, Worship, Fellowship, Service/Compassion. This dose of reality is enough usually for significant growth in many of these categories. This is just letting measured reality drive us toward better accomplishment of God's purposes for ministry.

Once people clearly know what the reality is and what the purposes are then they can pray and dream with God about what God might want to do that is shocking, wonderful, and glorifying to Him. So I put the vision chapter first because of its power and once you are awakened to it, you will be ten times the better leader that you were before you embraced vision as a minister. But then you will need to put reality consistently ahead of vision in the application of these skills.

Gaining Reality in Your Ministry

In this section I will give you projects, surveys, and tests in each of the four categories (objectives, strategies, people, and resources). It may be depressing at first, but answers will grow out of this dose of reality. First let's take an overall survey of your ministry. If you are leading a ministry like children's or student's, you want to take this survey twice: once on the whole church and then again for your specific ministry.

Church Health Survey

There are ten systems operating in every ministry and the health of those systems creates the health of the whole ministry. This survey will identify a ministry's top two systems and bottom two systems. A focus on the bottom two systems for a year will usually result in the greatest change in the health of the ministry. To maximize the validity of the survey, have at least twenty-five people in the ministry take the survey. THE L.E.A.D.E.R.S.H.O.P. SYSTEM	0 = never 1 = rarely 3 = sometimes 5= regularly 8 = usually 10 = always
1. This ministry is healthy and vibrant.	0 1 3 5 8 10
2. This ministry has compelling specific goals for the next few years and mobilizes people to accomplish them.	0 1 3 5 8 10
3. This ministry leads people to faith in Christ.	0 1 3 5 8 10
4. Each major event is promoted at least seven different ways.	0 1 3 5 8 10
5. This ministry changes people's lives.	0 1 3 5 8 10
6. This ministry regularly recruits and deploys new people into serving in the church.	0 1 3 5 8 10

7. This ministry spends money on life transformation, new converts, tangible help to the poor, deep connection between Christians, and increasing God's reputation and glory.	0 1 3 5 8 10
8. The worship services of this ministry consistently enrapture people in God's presence and exalt His name.	0 1 3 5 8 10
9. People in this ministry are filled up emotionally, spiritually, relationally, and mentally by their involvement.	0 1 3 5 8 10
10. This church aims all of its programs at exalting God, transforming people's lives, reaching new people with the gospel, deep connection between Christians, or tangible evidence of God's love to the less fortunate.	0 1 3 5 8 10
11. The average person could state the five reasons for the church.	0 1 3 5 8 10
12. This ministry raises up at least six to ten new godly leaders every year.	0 1 3 5 8 10
13. Evangelism is a high priority in this ministry.	0 1 3 5 8 10
14. On a person's first visit they are welcomed and made to feel comfortable by at least six different people in various parts of the facility.	0 1 3 5 8 10
15. This ministry produces a mature Christian after a certain period of time; a transformed person after a long term exposure to the ministry.	0 1 3 5 8 10
16. This ministry trains people to do ministry effectively.	0 1 3 5 8 10
17. This ministry has people regularly give tithes and offerings to help advance the life transformational ministries of the church.	0 1 3 5 8 10

18. This ministry shows people how to draw near to God each week.	0 1 3 5 8 10
19. The community knows that God loves them through this ministry.	0 1 3 5 8 10
20. It is clear who has decision-making authority over each ministry and person.	0 1 3 5 8 10
21. The ministry leaders pray and plan the ministry's specific goals and not uninvolved people.	0 1 3 5 8 10
22. People know what the specific goals are for the next twelve months.	0 1 3 5 8 10
23. This ministry uses a variety of ways to present the gospel.	0 1 3 5 8 10
24. The visitor is warmly contacted by the church at least six different times in the first two weeks.	0 1 3 5 8 10
25. Every week the instruction in this ministry causes people to apply the Bible to their lives.	0 1 3 5 8 10
26. This ministry helps people uncover their "gifted" ministry place.	0 1 3 5 8 10
27. This ministry uses its present facilities wisely.	0 1 3 5 8 10
28. This ministry is very effective at praying and seeing God answer.	0 1 3 5 8 10
29. People develop deep friendships in this ministry.	0 1 3 5 8 10
30. The paid ministerial staff produce excellence in children's ministry, weekend services, youth ministries, and adult ministries.	0 1 3 5 8 10
31. The programs and sub-ministries actually accomplish the purposes of the ministry.	0 1 3 5 8 10

32. Pastors and leaders read books, listen to tapes, and attend conferences to keep learning.	0 1 3 5 8 10
33. This ministry trains its members on how to witness effectively.	0 1 3 5 8 10
34. In their first year, a visitor has been invited to the pastor's home, become a part of a small group, attended some classes on how the church and Christianity works, has three new friends, and serves the church in some way.	0 1 3 5 8 10
35. People in this ministry practice their faith during the week.	0 1 3 5 8 10
36. The leaders of this ministry delegate whole sections of ministry to people they have raised up.	0 1 3 5 8 10
37. This ministry plans ahead for future facility needs.	0 1 3 5 8 10
38. God's blessing and presence is all over this ministry.	0 1 3 5 8 10
39. This ministry cares for the unlovely, afflicted, oppressed, and poor.	0 1 3 5 8 10
40. Decisions are clear and made to promote worship, discipleship, evangelism, fellowship, and compassion; not pet programs and personal agendas.	0 1 3 5 8 10
41. This ministry is innovative but not gimmick or fad driven.	0 1 3 5 8 10

UNDERSTANDING YOUR MINISTRY SCORE

There are ten systems operating in every ministry. Each of the systems was given four questions in this survey. By adding up the questions from each system you can determine your score for that system. You are looking to identify your two strongest systems and your two weakest systems. You will be tempted to try and work on all of the systems at once; this is unwise and usually results in little if any progress. Instead, identify your two weakest systems and focus attention, resources, and change in these two areas and the ministry will see the greatest improvement. As the church grows, the survey results will change and systems will need attention at this new size.

THE L.E.A.D.E.R.S.H.O.P. SYSTEM

The Leadership System	Questions 2, 12, 22, 32
The Evangelism System	Questions 3, 13, 23, 33
The Assimilation System	Questions 4, 14, 24, 34
The Discipleship System	Questions 5, 15, 25, 35
The Equipping System	Questions 6, 16, 26, 36
The Resources System	Questions 7, 17, 27, 37
The Spiritual System	Questions 8, 18, 28, 38
The Heart System	Questions 9, 19, 29, 39
The Organizational System	Questions 10, 20, 30, 40
The Purpose System	Questions 11, 21, 31, 41
Overview of all ministry systems	

Check out all the ministry resources at the Principles to Live By website www.ptlb.com.

How was your first dose of reality? Invigorating, I hope. Now let's go a little deeper. How is your ministry doing at the objectives of the church? Realize that it is very easy for a church to become a social club and not accomplish the purposes that Christ established for it. In my experience it takes about six months to a year for a church to drift from effectiveness to going through the motions. So I recommend that every six months to one year leaders ask and answer some rather pointed questions about whether the ministry achieved Jesus' objectives for the church. In my understanding, the objectives of the church are evangelism, discipleship, worship, fellowship, and compassion/service. Look at how God puts it in Acts 2:42 as the early church began to function.

They were continually devoting themselves to the apostles' teaching and to fellowship, to the breaking of bread and to prayer. Everyone kept feeling a sense of awe; and many wonders and signs were taking place through the apostles. And all those who had believed were together and had all things in common; and they began selling their property and possessions and were sharing them with all, as anyone might have need. Day by day continuing with one mind in the temple, and breaking bread from house to house, they were taking their meals together with gladness and sincerity of heart, praising God and having favor with all the people. And the Lord was adding to their number day by day those who were being saved.

Worship

One of the prime objectives for the church is to exalt, magnify, and praise God the Father, God the Son, and God the Holy Spirit in as large a way as possible. This means that inviting people into a worship experience is one of the objectives of the church. This includes conducting corporate worship services and instructing how to have private worship. True Christian worship is a life-changing experience of communication and connection with God. It matters how many people come to worship God and how deeply people are drawn into worship at that service. Therefore, two crucial questions that must be asked and answered are

How many people came to worship this week?

How many people connected and communicated with God at worship this week?

Most churches keep track of attendance at the worship services as that is a measure of their success. It is good to have the reality of the attendance numbers, but it is also crucial that some form of reality on the second question is also achieved. The church must ask the second question from the perspective, "We put on a worship service this last week, and X number of people came." "How many of those who came were transported into the presence of God and worshipped Him and heard from Him because of the worship service that we put on?" If that number is very low then while the first number may be high, it can so easily become just a show for the audience instead of praise for the King of Kings.

Once a year or twice a year, ask people to respond to a one or two question survey about this second question. Usually a slip of paper in the bulletin that people can anonymously respond and drop in the offering plate is best. An online survey can also be effective and helpful.

I feel the most connected to God in the worship service during: Singing - Offering/Communion – Special Music/Guests – Preaching - Prayer

What percent of people are tuned in to God during the worship service? 20% - 30% - 40% - 50% - 60% - 70% - 80% - 90% - 100%

If you don't do this, then every leader in the church will evaluate the effectiveness of the worship service by whether they liked it or whether they were brought into the presence of God. This is not an accurate way to measure the effectiveness of a worship service.

Let me tell you a story of a church I visited where the pastor came to the church in the early 1980's. He was a product of the 1970's contemporary Christian scene. When I visited the church in 2004, it was like I entered into a time tunnel and landed in 1979. The music, flow, and preaching were perfect for that era. It was perfect for the pastor. It was just the way he wanted to worship. The problem was that fewer and fewer people enjoyed that particular style of worship. He was at a loss as to why his church was on the decline. He had failed to realize that just because he liked worship a particular way, lots of other people did not connect with God through that style of worship. Unfortunately, he refused to admit that his view was myopic and kept doing it the way he liked, and now the church is down to less than forty people.

Evangelism

The church must embrace the fact that one of its most significant purposes for existence is helping people find God through Jesus Christ. There are really only a few questions to ask in the area of evangelism. The essential question that must be asked is: **How many people became Christians last year in your ministry?** Every ministry in the church needs to come up with a number. In many cases when you start asking this question the answer will be ZERO. Whatever the number is this establishes a baseline for the next year. Can we improve at evangelism and have more people make professions of faith next year? You can if it is an objective. You can't if you don't aim at it.

Some churches keep track of new Christians differently than others -- some keep track of professions of faith; others keep track of baptisms. However your church keeps track of people becoming Christian is fine. But you must start aiming at that happening more often in your church by keeping track of when it happens.

A second question that is helpful is: **How many presentations of the gospel were made last year?** Was it presented in the main worship service each week? Was the gospel presented at the student gatherings? Were the children presented with the gospel in their Sunday school classes? Were the seniors given the chance to respond to the gospel in their outings and gatherings? It often becomes really clear that more people did not become Christians last year because we did not offer the gospel to them. With this information you can see what parts of the ministry is making presentations of the gospel and how many presentations of the gospel are typically needed before one person becomes a Christian in your church.

A third question that is interesting is to divide the number of new Christians by the annual budget. This is what it costs God through your church to make a new Christian. If you have a budget of $300,000 and you had five new Christians last year, then it costs you $60,000 to produce one new Christian. This is always a humbling but instructive figure.

One of the reasons that churches should go through this exercise is because Christians can so easily focus inward and forget that we have the light of the world and the only hope for reconciliation with God, Jesus Christ. The church often can become a social club for people we already know, and we can abandon the lost and dying world. Don't let this happen to your church and your ministry. Ask the hard questions about evangelism.

Fellowship

A third objective for the church is to connect people in increasingly transparent spiritual relationships with other Christians. People need other Christians helping them along in the journey of faith. A Lone Ranger Christian is not going to make it.

There are generally two ways of gauging fellowship. First, a church can keep track of who and how many are becoming church members. Second, the church can keep track of people who are in some form of authentic community in the church. Therefore the church needs to help people find Christians who can walk the life of faith with them. Real authentic fellowship with sincere Christians is a key life-giving element in life. Therefore a crucial question must be asked and answered:

How many people in this church were in an increasingly transparent spiritual relationship with other Christians last year?

There are a number of ways to get this information. Most churches just assume that if a person is in a small group or Sunday school class, then they are having fellowship. This may or may not be the case. Again you can potentially discern the answer through a simple survey done on Sunday morning or online. The questions could be very basic such as

In this last year were you involved in an increasingly transparent spiritual relationship with other Christians at this church? Yes / No

In the last year I have prayed with other Christians at this church. Daily – Weekly - Monthly – Once - Never

This number can then be compared with how many people are in small groups and Sunday school classes to see how effective those groups are at providing fellowship.

Let me also suggest a more extensive fellowship questionnaire. This could also be given during the worship service and/or online. Some churches do this type of extensive survey through their small groups. This unfortunately leaves out those who do not attend small groups.

One can also adapt the engaged employee survey that is used by the Gallup organization. With very little adaptation, its twelve questions get to the heart of real fellowship. These can be found in Marcus Buckingham and Curt Coffman's book, *First Break all the Rules.*

Discipleship

Another objective for the church is to grow people in the love and knowledge of the Savior. This includes three basic areas of increasing knowledge and action: how to love Him, understanding Christian truth, and how to live Christ's way in every area of life. Discipleship deals with life transformation. Therefore people should be changing in what they know and how they live. The question that must be asked and answered is: **How many people have grown in their Christian life this year?**

Unfortunately many churches have no way of tracking this crucial objective. Most churches that do measure discipleship do it in an indirect way by asking: **How many people were involved in a Christian discipleship group this last year?** This number then becomes the baseline for the next year to see if an increasing number of people are growing as Christians. This indirect measure is good but is most helpful if it is followed up periodically with some form of individual survey to determine if people are actually changing in their behavior and knowledge.

Some churches will directly ask the people in the congregation if they have grown or survey them about their Christian life to see if there has been growth. Let me include a brief discipleship survey at this point that covers the three main areas of Christian discipleship: love for God, knowledge of Christian truth, love for self and others.

Love for God

What spiritual disciplines do you practice?	How often do you practice them?
Confession	Daily, Weekly, Monthly
Holy Spirit guidance and/or wisdom	Daily, Weekly, Monthly
Bible study	Daily, Weekly, Monthly
Prayer	Daily, Weekly, Monthly
Witnessing	Daily, Weekly, Monthly
Service	Daily, Weekly, Monthly
Private worship of God	Daily, Weekly, Monthly
Corporate worship of God (church service)	Daily, Weekly, Monthly
Memorization of scripture	Daily, Weekly, Monthly
Biblical meditation	Daily, Weekly, Monthly
Communion	Daily, Weekly, Monthly
Giving	Daily, Weekly, Monthly
Fellowship with other Christians	Daily, Weekly, Monthly
Love	Daily, Weekly, Monthly

Knowledge of Christian Truth

Basic Christian Truth (Doctrines)	What three Bible verses describe what you know about this Christian truth?
Bible	
God	
Jesus	
Holy Spirit	
Sin	
Salvation	
Church	
Angels	
Mankind	
Heaven, Hell, Judgment Day	
End Times	

Love for Self and Others

Relationships that need biblical love from you	What three to five specific biblical actions you do to show Christian love to
Yourself	
Your spouse	
Your family	
The people at work	
The people at church	
Your finances	
Your community and the world	
Your friends	
Your enemies	

Willow Creek Association has done the most extensive discipleship survey: the Reveal Survey. This survey can be very helpful and can be taken online (www.willowcreek.com).

Compassion/Service

The final objective for the church is to engage people in serving God inside the church and out in the world. This means that the church must aim at producing people who give of their time, energy, and talents for the love of God to be spread abroad. A church that is healthy has an increasing number of people giving time at the church and in the community. Too often churches are coddling the saved instead of mobilizing them for kingdom expansion. This means that two crucial questions that must be asked and answered are

How many people serve the Lord weekly in the church?

How many people from this church serve the Lord monthly in the community/world?

If a church is not able to mobilize its people to give of themselves to the various righteous causes that are all around them, then the church is unhealthy. In the church I pastored we talked about giving a minimum of two hours per week at church and two hours a month in the community. This was a basic rule of thumb for a healthy Christian life. Many Christians do this because the love of Christ inside of them impels them, but there is no encouragement coming from the church to volunteer along these lines. This is a shame. The church must start measuring their ability to mobilize people.

Strategies and Systems

Every church was originally set up to accomplish the five basic objectives of ministry. Those individuals who started the church probably began using the accepted systems, methods, and strategies of their day to accomplish evangelism, discipleship, worship, fellowship, and service. What often happens is that churches mistake the system or method for the goal. When this happens, a church is stuck as soon as the method they are using stops working. Take for example the church that started in the late 1960's and embraced the bus ministry as the key strategy to do evangelism. If the leaders of that church are still pushing bus evangelism in the new millennium, then they have confused a strategy for the objective. Therefore the systems, methods, and strategies that a church uses should be examined to see if they are still the best way to accomplish the five purposes. Can the systems be improved? When we look at the strategy objectively, is it still effective?

One of the best ways to begin examining strategy is to write down what is being done to accomplish the objectives for each ministry. I have found it very instructive to actually see the various things a ministry is doing on one chart. Ask each of the major ministries (typically a life stage that is responsible for all five objectives) to fill out a one-page chart detailing their methods or strategies for accomplishing Christ's purposes. It is always a humbling process for a church to have nothing in one or two of the categories for a particular life stage. There are over fifty percent of the churches in America that have no strategies for evangelism or compassion for adult ministry except hope. There are thousands of churches that have no strategies for worship except singing and preaching.

When you first start looking at reality it can be discouraging, but reality will usually cause some people to think of new ideas, new methods that might allow the church to achieve its God-given potential. Therefore this exercise in reality is needed.

This is the chart that I use to help ministries evaluate the strategies they are using.

What are you doing to cause people to Worship God currently?

What are you doing to cause Evangelism to take place currently?

What are you doing to make Fellowship happen currently?

What are you doing to cause Discipleship currently?

What are you doing to cause Service/Compassion to increase in your church currently?

Please feel free to make copies of this chart and use it.

Worship Matthew 4:10	Evangelism Matthew 4:19	Fellowship John 13:34, 35	Discipleship Matthew 28:18-20	Service / Compassion Matthew 5:45-48

People

Every church is about people and needs people to do its ministry. With the right people in the right leadership slots, the church explodes with health and growth. The wrong people in the wrong leadership positions doom a church. Therefore one of the critical realities of a church is

Who do we have in the leadership positions at this church?
Are they the right people?
Are they in the right positions?

Where do we need new leaders?
What kind of leaders do we need in these new positions?

Go ahead and actually answer the above questions. Don't just read them and think that you will be back to this exercise. Do it now. Put the answers on a separate sheet of paper or in this book itself. It does not matter if you already are thinking about changes in leadership. Just answer the reality questions right now.

Another crucial people question that is often overlooked in church work is whether the church is organized in the best way to achieve the objectives of the church and take advantage of the leaders at the church. Many times churches just keep doing church the way they have always done it without focusing on the objectives. Unfortunately a number of churches were organized in the distant past and those organizational patterns seem strange and unwieldy for people. Therefore it is important to ask:

What is the actual organization chart and reporting relationships now?

Are their ways to improve the organization to accomplish the objectives?

Are their ways to improve the organizational relationships to take advantage of the leaders that are on the team?

Resources

The final crucial reality that leaders must understand is the resources that are available to them. In church, these resources can be scarce and/or hidden from view. "You can have as much resources as you can raise" is the old adage that frightens many church leaders. It would seem obvious, but I have seen churches have to shut their doors because the leader does not have a grip on reality in regards to how much money is coming into the church. Some immature pastors plan and spend like it doesn't matter how much is presently coming in. Occasionally, God does provide the miracle in a last minute gift but not always. It is much better when the leader knows: here is how much has been coming in; here is how much we are expecting to come in; here is what we would do with any monies above the expected amount. Therefore the following two questions are critical:

What resources do you have to accomplish W E F D C

Per week

Per month

Per year

Where is the money going now?

What resources do you really need to accomplish W E F D C

> **Per week**

> **Per month**

> **Per year**

The second skill of great leadership is to ***define reality clearly***, even though it may be very painful and humbling. This means that the leader(s) must regularly assess: 1) the current attainment of the objectives; 2) the current strategies to attain those objectives; 3) the current people and their organization in accomplishing the objectives; 4) and, finally, the resources currently available and their allocation for accomplishing the objectives. If you have not done the assessments suggested in this chapter, go back and do them. Do not keep reading. The value of this book will be in doing the exercises and the creativity that will come from doing them. Please see the blank chart on the next page that allows you to put the present ministry reality on one sheet of paper. Each separate life stage ministry should fill out one of these ministry reality evaluations.

Ministry Reality

One of these charts should be filled out for each life stage ministry of the church.

Worship Matthew 4:10	Evangelism Matthew 4:19	Fellowship John 13:34, 35	Discipleship Matthew 28:18-20	Service / Compassion Matthew 5:45-48

LEADERSHIP SKILL #3 - RECRUIT NEXT-LEVEL PEOPLE

"The only thing that is keeping us from the fulfillment of great work is the employment of great leaders."
(Dr. Rich Frazer, President of S.O.S. Ministries)

Introduction

Pastors and Christian leaders must develop the ability to recruit and hire next-level leaders. Without increasingly strong sub-leaders, a ministry is doomed to stagnation and eventual decline. This chapter is about how to identify, recruit, and/or hire next-level leaders for ministry.

In the early days of my pastorate I was overjoyed when the board allowed me to use the little surplus we had gathered to hire a youth pastor. We were growing as a church, but our youth group was very weak. I reached out to a young man that I knew who was sharp and gifted. He agreed to become our new youth pastor. He was going to build a youth group of hundreds of people. Unfortunately, he did not have skills for drawing and collecting young people to a church. I had made my first hiring mistake. Two years of working with this sharp young man teaching, directing, and sending him to conferences did nothing. It was a bad hire on my part. He was not a bad guy. On the contrary he was a great guy who worked hard and got along well at the church, but he could not grow a youth group. He needed to move on to a place where his skills could really work. I needed to admit I had made a mistake and let him go. He moved on and it took the church a few years before they were willing to trust me with a full-time hire again. I learned a valuable lesson in leadership of a church. The people you hire must be able to take their ministry area to the next level or you shouldn't hire them. Let me say that again. The only reason a new staff person should be recruited or hired is that this person can take a ministry area to the next level whatever that next level looks like. Never hire people who can manage what you already have. Hire people who will drive the ministry area forward.

The problem is that these "next level" people are not easy to find. There is no store downtown stocked with wonderful Children's Directors or Worship Leaders. There are lots of Christians who are nice people, brilliant thinkers, and even excellent managers but they cannot grow anything. The leader must be constantly looking to upgrade their team. This means training, recruiting, hiring, and firing. This is what leaders do. If you are unwilling to upgrade your team, then you have opted out of leadership and have become a manager of the present status quo.

Every pastor has made hiring and recruiting mistakes. You thought you were getting a winner but instead you got a whiner. What are the keys to recruiting and/or hiring well? Let me give you four overall keys.

1) You must become clear what the next level looks like for the area you are recruiting. In other words, you do not start with the people; you start with the objective. If this unknown person were to be successful, what will they have accomplished a year from now. Different people may go after that objective in different ways; but you, the recruiter and/or hirer, must be clear as to what a win looks like.

2) You must always go after next-level people rather than settle for good-for-now people. Too many pastors and church leaders start with the people who are available. That is why step one is so essential. What are we trying to accomplish? Then it is easier to go after people who will be able to accomplish that objective. The great danger is that you will be sidetracked by good people who are available. Every great leader I know has been willing to overlook friends and competent available people waiting until they see the next-level leader that they are needing.

3) You must be willing to ask next-level people to join your team. Many pastors recruit and hire as though they are a beggar asking for a few scraps. Pastors and Christian leaders must realize that they are offering the opportunity to work directly for the advancement of the Kingdom of God. We are offering people the chance to change people's lives forever. It is a privilege to be asked to volunteer at the church, let alone be hired by the church. The pastor must ask busy, high energy, successful people to do something that really matters. If you can only approach people who are desperate or available, then you the leader have a problem you must correct. Learn to ask next-level people.

4) You must develop a good system for identifying next-level people. Every leader must go beyond a gut level feeling about a person and have some objective standards, tests, and evaluations that have proven to work in identifying next-level people. Let me add that you will never get recruiting and hiring right every time but following these simple steps will increase the number of next-level leaders in your ministry.

The Bible and Next-Level Leadership

The story of Jethro and Moses' impending ministry burnout in Exodus 18:17-27 gives the biblical basis for different levels of leaders and their importance. Moses was wearing himself out hearing and deciding personally every single disagreement between people in the massive exodus. He was wearing down and the people were wearing down because they had to wait on Moses.

Moses' father-in-law said to him, "The thing that you are doing is not good. You will surely wear out, both yourself and these people who are with you, for the task is too heavy for you; you cannot do it alone. Now listen to me: I will give you counsel, and God be with you. You be the people's representative before God, and you bring the disputes to God, then teach them the statutes and the laws, and make known to them the way in which they are to walk and the work they are to do. Furthermore, you shall select out of all the people able men who fear God, men of truth, those who hate dishonest gain; and you shall place these over them as leaders of thousands, of hundreds, of fifties and of tens. Let them judge the people at all times; and let it be that every major dispute they will bring to you, but every minor dispute they themselves will judge. So it will be easier for you, and they will bear the burden with you. If you do this thing and God so commands you, then you will be able to endure, and all these people also will go to their place in peace". So Moses listened to his father-in-law and did all that he had said. Moses chose able men out of all Israel and made them heads over the people, leaders of thousands, of hundreds, of fifties and of tens. They judged the people at all times; the difficult dispute they would bring to Moses, but every minor dispute they themselves would judge. Then Moses bade his father-in-law farewell, and he went his way into his own land.

Moses needed leaders to help make the ministry load bearable for both the ministers and the people. One of the basic ideas of the story of Moses and Jethro and leadership is that different people can lead different numbers of people. Jethro delineates five different levels of leaders: those who can lead tens; those who can lead fifties; those who can lead hundreds; those who can lead thousands; those who can lead millions. (Leadership of millions is implied because that size leader, Moses, was already in place.) The various leadership levels mean that a particular leader can cause a certain number of people (ten plus, fifty plus, one-hundred plus, one thousand plus, one million plus) to act in the right direction. There is some debate whether Jethro is referring to the ability to lead family units or individuals. Either way the numerical breakdowns are helpful. The idea here is that a leader has the ability to attract, hold, and direct towards right actions groups of ten plus, groups of fifty plus, groups of one hundred plus, groups of one thousand plus, and/or groups of one million plus. This, therefore, establishes the idea of levels of leadership ability. Whatever level your ministry is operating at, if it is to grow it will need more next-level leaders to help it get there. This vignette also illustrates the fact that it is not just one leader that is needed; multiple leaders provide the healthiest organization.

It is quite clear that God, throughout the Old and New Testaments, selected the best leaders for the endeavors that He was launching. In Acts 13 He selected Barnabas and Saul to be the leaders of the new missionary endeavors even though they were the two key leaders at the church they served. God selects Joshua, David, Moses, Paul, and many others to be leaders of His plans because they can take His work to the next level. Wherever God is doing a great work He has a leader in the middle of it, channeling the power and grace of God into that project.

What is Recruiting Next-level People?

Recruiting next-level people means having thought through what the next level in a ministry area looks like and then scouting hard to find a skilled person who can take that ministry to that new place. Too often pastors and Christian leaders want to delegate the headache of a ministry area to anyone just so it does not land on their desk anymore. This usually results in a ministry stagnating and, in some cases, declining.

It is crucial to visualize the next level of the ministry – that may mean numerical growth; it may mean quality growth; it may mean new levels of technical equipment and skill; it may mean personal growth; it may mean experiential growth or any number of other directions. But a group can't go where at least one leader can't imagine the broad outlines of that future. Somebody must be able to describe the preferred future. Then it is possible to begin describing the kind of person who can get you there.

Next-level leaders are always busy. They aren't asking for things to do. They are already leading something else towards success and productivity. Next-level people are rarely available. They will need to be recruited, wooed, and drawn to your assignment. One of the key mistakes that pastors and Christian leaders make is looking for someone who is available rather than looking for someone who has the necessary skill, character, and chemistry to cause the needed growth and impact. Available people are often available for a reason; they were released from their last job. Never mistake an available person for the right person.

In my previous position as District Superintendent, I recommended that a particularly troubled church call a particular pastor. We will call him Pastor Tom. Pastor Tom was very quiet and loving and in many people's minds not at all what this contentious church needed. But I knew that underneath his loving and gentle exterior was a godly man who was clearly a next-level leader for this particular church. Almost from the moment that he stepped foot on the grounds of the church, the contentious spirit began dissipating, the quality of the ministry improved, and new families began attaching themselves to the church. The numerical growth of this church has not been bombastic; but it has been real and sustainable. Pastor Tom was a next-level leader for this ministry and continues to be one.

Is it possible for a present leader of a ministry to become a next-level leader? Yes and no. It is possible for a present leader to catch fire and lead a ministry to a new level of effectiveness if they grow as a person and as a leader. They must also have an accurate picture of what next level is like in their mind. The two crucial pieces are a willingness to constantly picture the next level of ministry in an area (rather than just deal with what is and its accompanying problems) and growing into the changes that will surely be needed to achieve that next level.

Many people are next-level people in some arena, but they have allowed themselves to become ineffective often through a lack of focus. Next-level people can become mediocre people by trying to do too much and not focusing their attention. Many great lay people have allowed themselves to be non-impact players for the Kingdom of God by being too busy. Focus on only a few things and make sure that you have time for a full personal, family, and relational life.

How Do You Recruit Next-level Leaders?

I am amazed at the number of pastors who are waiting for a next-level leader to walk into their church on a Sunday and announce that they are ready for whatever the pastor needs done. The sharp lay leader is not going to approach you after a Sunday message and say he was looking at investing ten to fifteen hours of his week in the church and $20,000 a year. This just doesn't happen anymore. If it ever did happen in the past, it rarely happens in the present. You, as the leader, must go get them. You must find them. You must recruit them. You may need to hire them. You must recruit them from within the church and from outside the church. The better leader they are, the more that they are already engaged in worthwhile causes.

Once I understood that the leaders I needed were not going to just show up, I stopped waiting and went out looking for these people. I started shamelessly interviewing Christians who lived or worked anywhere near our church. I once asked a sharp next-level couple who didn't attend our church to drive forty-five minutes to be a part of our church rather than continue sitting unused in their current church. I asked business men and women to give us ten to twenty hours of their time and make a difference for God. Yes, I got turned down a lot, but I also got enough "Yes" to change the nature of our church. I asked God to point out any leaders anywhere so that I could recruit them to this great cause of changing our community for Christ.

I have given this same advice to hundreds of pastors now; and I have watched them revolutionize their churches as they have gone out into the community, the schools, and businesses and asked next-level leaders to come help them. These people have come on as volunteers, part-timers, and even full-time ministers. If you are a leader you must constantly recruit leaders to your area of ministry. I remember hearing John Maxwell talk about having dozens of lunches each quarter with sharp young couples where he shared the vision of the church and recruited them into leadership in the church. The fact that he asked them to be a part of something bigger than themselves, in a number of cases, turned these people's lives around. Many times pastors are so focused on preaching the next sermon they do not allot time for recruiting leaders, and yet it is the recruiting of next-level leaders that will determine the size and health of the church far more than their sermon.

What is it that will cause them to want to be on your team? What are the ways that a next-level person can be drawn toward your project or ministry? Let me suggest that any and all of the following incentives may work on a next-level leader:

Ô   the power of the cause
Ô   the need for more money for themselves or their family
Ô   the opportunity to be mentored

Ô   a new title
Ô   the size of the challenge
Ô   the direction of God
Ô   the need for a change from their current situation
Ô   the opportunity to learn new skills
Ô   the needs of the people being ministered to
Ô   stagnation in their present situation
Ô   the chance to impact more people or different people

Recruiting

Every church is constantly in the business of recruiting volunteers, so let's look more closely at the tried and true ways of recruiting. There are five classic ways of recruiting workers and leaders to the ministry of the church: announcements; classes; mandatory service; Ministry Fair; personal recruitment.

Announcements

Announcements are common to all churches and considered by many to be the only way to recruit volunteers. Announcements work best in small churches under a hundred people and become increasingly ineffective between 100 and 2,000. They do become a recruiting tool in 2,000 plus size churches when an all-church push is needed. Good announcements are like a good movie or good sermon: a clear and compelling statement or picture of the problem, difficulty, or crisis with a specific number of people volunteering for a specific assignment as the solution to the issue. Do not overuse church-wide announcements or they will become ineffective.

It is important to emphasize in church that there are two kinds of service in a church: "have to" ministry and "want to" ministry. In the present day the church must educate people that they need to serve in the church in order for the ministry to continue and to move forward. Too many people today feel that service organizations will just always exist, and that they do not have to help. People must also be given help in compartmentalizing their service at the church into the whole scheme of their life. I have found that giving people a general rule of thumb of two hours plus per week in the church and two hours per month in the community really helps. This allows people to mentally realize that serving in the church will not take over their life. Obviously many people will serve more than this, but it is the baseline of minimum health in your service.

Classes

Classes are becoming a common way to help people find their way into serving in the church. Classes help a person find their sweet spot in ministry which is a crucial function in the discipleship process. Classes help a person find their "want to" ministry but are not always effective at mobilizing large numbers of volunteers. Therefore classes must be one of the ongoing strategies in a church and not the only strategy for helping people start serving. The most helpful recruiting tool from classes is to have people from the various ministry areas of the church describe their ministry and the opportunities in that part of the church. The people in the class can then ask questions and probe further about an area of ministry that they are interested in. The ministries should have sign-up sheets where people can give their name and contact information for ministries that they want to jump into and try. Take time in the class for people to sign up.

Ministry Fairs

Ministry Fairs are the new darling of larger churches and can effectively motivate people to find their place of service in the church. A Ministry Fair is usually an event at the church. A sermon is preached about the need for serving with the application being to go out to the lobby or patio and explore all the various ministry opportunities in the church. The sermon should be shorter than the typical sermon by at least ten minutes so people feel that they have time to explore the booths. Each separate ministry in the church should have a booth with sign-up sheets, brochures, pictures, job openings and people to talk with. The whole atmosphere of the Ministry Fair should be fun and exciting. Many churches have found that food booths and even game booths mixed into the various service opportunities keep the atmosphere light and enjoyable. In order for the Ministry Fair to be maximally effective, the staff of each individual ministry must personally follow up and recruit the people who sign up.

Some churches will spend a whole month in a Ministry Fair mode talking, recruiting, and upholding the value of service. Some churches do Ministry Fairs in August to get ready for the coming school year and ministry year. Some churches have taken to doing the Ministry Fair push in May or June for a September start. These churches explain that this allows them to spend the whole summer following up, recruiting, and training. Many people do find it easier to volunteer when the commitment doesn't start for three months.

Mandatory Service

At one church I visited, the Children's Director asked us to pray for her as she was so busy. We asked why she was so busy. She replied that she had too many people signing up to help in children's ministry and was having training meeting after training meeting to equip all these people. I was immediately curious, so I asked what she was doing to recruit people to her ministry. She said that when someone put their child in children's ministries, they would fill out the information sheet and she added a second sheet which was a sheet full of the various jobs that could be done in children's ministry. It ran the gamut from one hour a month to ten hours per week. It simply stated that since they had their child participating in the children's program, they were expected to serve somewhere in the ministry. The only exception was if they were serving in another ministry of the church already. I know of a number of churches – both large and small – that use this method for their children's ministry.

This somewhat controversial way of recruiting people into service is to require that everyone serve somewhere in the church. If they attend, they will be called to serve. It is an expectation. Requiring people to serve in a ministry is used in a number of churches, but it usually is restricted to the children's and nursery ministries. This approach is used in a number of volunteer organizations – both secular and religious. If your child participates in the organization, then you need to do your part of the work. Usually the information that is provided when a child or teen is registered into a ministry is used to contact the parents. The parents are then asked which of a myriad of service opportunities they would like to be help with.

Personal Recruitment

Personal recruitment is still one of the most effective ways of recruiting people into service in the church. Some form of personal recruitment will always be needed even if the other means are working to some degree. The larger the church, the more personal recruitment will be needed for the leadership positions. Many people shy away from personally asking someone directly if they will serve in their ministry. This is unfortunate because the rewards of jumping in are so powerful. We must get over our reluctance to ask people to get involved. I have often called this the Big Ask. Leaders just must be comfortable doing this. If you are in a church under five-hundred people, you will need to spend time doing this every single week or you will constantly suffer a shortage of help in the crucial ministries of the church. I realize that many pastors and Christian leaders shy away from asking people to give up some of their time and abilities to help the church because they are already so busy with the rest of life. But church work is important and quality people need to do it. Yes, people are busy but there are significant rewards for serving God in His church. There is nothing as exhilarating as ministering to another person and changing their life for the good. You are not burdening people with another thing. You are offering them an opportunity to engage in the work of God, meet new people, change people's lives, and do eternally significant work. Serving God is a part of a balanced life. If they are not serving, then they are living an unbalanced life. If they are not serving, they are using that time for some destructive or counterproductive pursuit.

Let me give you an example of personal recruitment at its best. In the final five years of my tenure at Twin Lakes Community Church, the children's ministry in our church was by far the most successful at recruiting people. The other ministries were complaining that the children's department always stole their best prospects and that there were not enough volunteers to go around. After trying to deal with this issue on a number of levels, I finally asked our Children's Ministry Director to come tell us how she went about recruiting people. She taught all of us what her ministry did to recruit people. Everyone on staff compared what they were doing with what the children's ministry did and some even suggested ways to potentially improve the Children Director's method. I was then able to tell all of our departments that they now knew the gold standard for recruiting. Use this system and stop complaining.

Here is her system:

1. Pray through the Ministry Fair list and/or the church directory and visitors list asking God to show you who might be a good fit for your area of ministry.

2. Call the people God puts on your mind immediately. Don't wait. Call and leave a message if they are not home and let them know that you wanted to talk with them.

3. When you talk with them, let them know about the wonderful opportunities in your area of ministry.

4. Tell them that you don't want them to give you an answer right away. You really would like to know if they would pray about being a part of your area of ministry. If God says no, then fine. But if God says, give it a try, then they should let you know in a few days.

5. Follow up the conversation in a few days, by phone, email, or personal appointment. The higher the level of leadership, the more a personal appointment follow up is necessary.

Many churches over one-thousand in attendance are setting up a volunteer central position where a leader and a team make these phone calls every week rather than the individual ministry leader personally. These calls are made to new visitors, uninvolved members, and regular attenders. This is often a part of the assimilation or connections ministry.

Hiring Next-Level Leaders

In order for a church to grow in size, strength, and depth the current leaders must grow and new leaders must be added who can take the church to a new level of effectiveness and impact. Both of these things must happen or the church will plateau or decline. Make sure that you are growing and that you hire next-level leaders. There are three crucial steps when hiring a next-level staff person.

Ô Write down what the requirements, objectives, and rewards of the position before you start looking at candidates.
Ô Publish your need for a leader until you have three to five next-level leader candidates.
Ô Thoroughly evaluate the three to five potential next-level leader candidates.
  o Use the 4 C's as an evaluation tool
  o Use the 4 E and 1P evaluation system
  o Use the Jethro-Moses leadership levels as a system
  o Use multiple interviews
  o Use background and reference checks

Hire a next-level leader and let them do their thing.

Let me tell you the story of Pastor Ralph. Pastor Ralph was excited. He was going to hire a staff person who would allow the church to rocket forward in size, depth, and energy. I asked who the prospective, dynamic staff person was who would do all these things. He told me about Pastor Ted and his wife. I knew Pastor Ted from previous encounters and was doubtful that he would help any church. He was at best a leader of ten, maybe twenty. I asked Pastor Ralph what he was looking to accomplish through hiring Pastor Ted. He told me that he wanted to see the youth group double and the children's ministry grow by almost triple. "Did he really think that Pastor Ted and his wife would accomplish those goals?" He replied, "Yes." I told him that his goals were the right goals, but that everything I knew about Pastor Ted told me that this young man would never be able to fulfill Pastor Ralph's dreams.

Pastor Ralph was so excited about getting a staff person that he did not do all the work he should have. He hired him anyway and suffered through two years of ineffective ministry and extra mentoring that changed nothing. Eventually Pastor Ralph had to let Pastor Ted go. There was great relief when they finally left and the church was smaller than when Pastor Ted was hired. Staff hiring mistakes are the constant bane of every pastor/leader over one-hundred people. Go after next-level leaders. You will never get it right every time, but there are ways to make the right hire more often.

An overriding truth that every great leader in any field knows is that the team with the best players wins. There are rare exceptions, but in almost every case the team with the best players wins. Therefore, one of the absolutely key things that the leader must spend time on is getting the best people to play for his/her team. One cannot win consistently without this. A good leader will spend a considerable amount of time, energy, and resources evaluating, recruiting, and retaining the best players.

Unfortunately, many pastors have a mindset that they will wait to see who comes through the door of the church and make do with the people that "God has sent." I even find pastors who are hoping God will send better leaders to the church but not doing what is necessary to go find better leaders. Pastors must open their eyes and see that it is their responsibility to hire the best staff members. Obviously there is the approval and input that is needed from the appropriate committees and leaders but go get the best people and you will be surprised at how much of a difference it makes.

A second truth that leaders know is that great leaders constantly upgrade their team. Great staff people move on to other churches; some staff need to be let go for violating the rules; some staff people need to be reassigned because they cannot meet the requirements of the position. So the leader in church must be constantly looking to upgrade the effectiveness of their team through new hires.

The following is a step-by-step process for making sure that you hire the best players – next -level people. Work through all the steps and you will be surprised at the quality of the people you will have to hire.

Step #1   Write down what the requirements, objectives, and rewards of the position are before you start looking at candidates

What is the position?

What are the objectives for the position?
- Ô   What are the attendance objectives?
- Ô   What are the financial objectives?
- Ô   What are the evangelistic objectives?
- Ô   What are the discipleship – life transformation objectives?
- Ô   What are the worship/prayer objectives?
- Ô   What are the fellowship objectives?
- Ô   What are the compassion objectives?
- Ô   What are the organizational objectives?

What are the requirements of the position?
- Ô   What are the minimum experience requirements?
- Ô   What are the minimum education requirements?
- Ô   What are the technological requirements?

What is the salary and benefits range of this position?
- Ô   Salary range
- Ô   Benefits
- Ô   Bonus
- Ô   Perks

What is the length of the contract?
- Ô How long is the probation period?
- Ô How often is the evaluation and/or review of work done?

What gifts and abilities are required for this position?

What are the reporting relationships of this position?
- Ô Who does this person report to?
- Ô Who reports to this person?
- Ô Who are their colleagues?
- Ô What teams is this person on?

What are their first, second and third teams?

Describe the ideal next-level leader for this position?

What is their minimum educational level?

Describe the character for a leader who fills this position.

What is their level of experience?

What are their talents, gifts, abilities, and passions?

What are the personality traits of the leader who fills this position?

What are the ministry and life objectives of this leader?

What is the preferred attitude of the leader who fills this position?

It is important to get input from a number of sources as you put together this profile of the position and the ideal candidate. When a number of people on staff, on the board, and in the congregation are giving input, then the picture of what is really needed will more clearly emerge.

If you write down what the position is all about and what the expectations are for the person who fills this position before you start looking, you will usually not be as swayed by who happens to be available. It is too easy to bend what you were looking for toward the people you find if you don't have it written down. Remember that every position you are hiring for has a set of objectives that you want that person to accomplish. This is true even if you don't have it all written down. It is best to write down what you are thinking and have other people look at your ideas and react to them. There are a number of benefits to writing down what you want the person to achieve: the objectives will be clearer; more people will have input on the position; the candidates will be clearer on what is expected.

Too many churches have made the mistake of saying, "We need a Youth Pastor." "Let's go get one." "Everybody knows what a Youth Pastor does." "Would you like to be our Youth Pastor?" The candidate agrees to become the Youth Pastor and the hidden expectations for this position come pouring out after they have been hired while they believed that they would get to design their own program. This whole problem would be avoided if the expectations were written down ahead of time so everyone could see what is being offered and expected.

Step #2 Publish the need for a leader until you get three to five next-level leaders as candidates.

Many pastors tell me that they would hire a next-level leader if they knew any. They ask me to show them where they all are. There is no store where you can go browse through isle after isle of great Worship Pastors or Children's Directors. It takes work to find a next-level leader. Most churches fail to hire a next-level leader because they do not get enough quality applicants. Too often churches depend upon coincidence and internal church networks to suggest who to hire. This method will rarely allow you to find a next-level leader. Just because you heard of a guy who could do that job from your brother-in-law doesn't make him a next-level leader nor God's choice for the position. Decide what you need for the position and start an aggressive search for the kind of person that you need to lead that area of ministry to the next level. If the job is not published to a large enough group(s), then the church will not see who they could have hired.

Advertise (get the word out) your interest in filling a position in the appropriate places. Advertise in the church, on the Internet, on your web page, with local colleges, seminaries, and employment boards and organizations. In order to get the best candidates – and more importantly the right candidates – you need to cast a wide net about the job. Be willing to let people know in a number of different ways that your church has a position. Yes, you will get people who are not qualified that apply, but you will get people who are wonderfully capable applying also.

Ask key leaders inside and outside the church who they know or could recommend for this position. This is one of the most profound suggestions in this book. It will revolutionize the pool of people you are evaluating. I have found that there are well-placed people (college and seminary professors, college presidents, teachers, executive pastors, business owners, etc.) who often know someone who is really sharp and might make a move, but they are not really looking. It is these kinds of people that can really make a huge difference in your ministry. The more crucial the leadership position, the more one needs to be diligent in pursuing those who are not really looking but might be willing to consider a move if the situation were right. These are called word-of-mouth recommendations. Many times this is the best way to uncover incredible next-level leaders. People who are doing a terrific job and are not looking to move are some of the most talented people you should consider.

There are times when you cannot, through normal means, find the right kind of candidates that you want. It is in these kinds of situations you may want to hire a person who does this for a living. These have been called **head hunting services** and can at times give you a good list of candidates. The head hunter will do what we just discussed in the previous two paragraphs, sometimes with an expanded list of key people to ask. While this service is relatively new in the church world, it does exist. The best candidates are many times not interested in working with each smaller church that might want to see if they can land the big fish, so they go through a head hunting service that will screen out the types of jobs that are of no interest to them.

Keep collecting names and resumés until there are three to five really good potential hires to pick from. Do not hire the first person who you run across who is sharp and capable. The only exception to this is if the leader is supremely talented and you might lose them. But this is a rare occurrence. You really don't know how sharp they are until you compare them with three to five equally sharp people who can do the job at the level you want. A viable candidate is someone who has significant experience growing to or performing at the level you desire. You want the choice to come down to chemistry or philosophy and not competence. You do not want to be choosing from one good and ten mediocre people. Your feeling should be that any one of the top five people would do a terrific job.

Once the determination has been made that a candidate is in the not-a-chance pile, do not consider them again. Send them a note thanking them for their submission, but you are going in a different direction at this time.

Step #3 Thoroughly evaluate the three to five potential next-level leader candidates and hire the best fit using the four C's evaluation system.

Check the potential leaders thoroughly. Whatever systems you use to understand a person, those systems need to tell you everything you need to know about the potential new hire. Give them personality tests, criminal checks, credit checks, and even psychological exams. You should not be surprised by their credit card debt. You should not be surprised by their talkative or dominating behavior. You should not be surprised by their food allergies. You should not be surprised by their unique habits or idiosyncrasies. You should know how well they work with teams and whether they can defer to others. It is crucial that you develop a thorough evaluation system that can accurately predict what a person will be like in the work environment.

I have put this process down as though it does not begin until after you have three to five great candidates, but this is not the actual way that these steps work. As soon as you uncover a potential next-level leader, begin the process of evaluating this person, even though you will be searching for others at the same time. This evaluation process is a way of screening out people who appear to be a great candidate but would not fit your ministry or would not really be able to meet your expectations.

The following is one way of evaluating a next-level leader. This is not the only way or even the best way; it is a way that I have found effective. It is a lot of work and so sometimes churches and leaders skip these steps and hire people without evaluating them thoroughly. The question that needs to be asked is: What does a next level person look like? They all have four constants in their life. They are full of Character, Competence, Chemistry, and Culture. There are a number of ways of determining whether a person has these or not. I have included a few different ways to evaluate these four crucial arenas.

Interview the candidate and their references thoroughly. Having a team of people conduct phone interviews from a prepared list of questions should bring out the candidates strengths and weaknesses. The references should be asked for others who might be called as to gain further insight into this person. Using the description of the position that was created earlier, a team of people should go over the objectives with the potential candidate to see how they would accomplish these objectives.

Have the candidates respond to a written set of questions. All candidates should respond to the same written set of questions. This gives you ways of comparing answers, style, writing ability, and attention to details. Written responses show you this person's ability to write and think in this medium. It is not uncommon to have a few different written lists of questions that would be given over a period of weeks or months. The candidate's ability to respond in a timely manner and the thoughtfulness of the answers communicate significant things about the potential candidate.

Continue progressing with interviewing (written, phone, and video) even as you collect more resumés. Some candidates will be ahead of others in the process. There does, however, need to be a deadline where you will no longer collect resumés. The collecting of resumés cannot be forever open-ended. There is a time to decide amongst the candidates who you have uncovered. I have watched churches and committees become so enamored with a particular television or popular preacher that they will not accept anyone except the legend as a candidate.

In hiring for some ministry positions, it is helpful to watch the candidate performing their ministry in their present setting. One of the options that can be very instructive is to have one or two people go to where the person is currently employed and watch them do their job. Lots of insights can be gained by watching a person go through their normal ministry day in their current position. Is their approach to ministry scalable? Do they have unique factors in their current settings that are accelerating or impeding growth? Do their mannerisms and personal appearance suggest that they would be a fit in your setting?

Bring them to your place and have them interviewed by different people. It is very helpful to have the candidate come to your church and react to the settings, facilities, and people that are in your town. A new set of questions for these interactions can be very helpful. Asking the candidate what they see. Asking them what is different from their present ministry. Asking them what they might change and what they might leave in place.

Let me repeat, again, that the person who is a great hire is a next-level leader for your ministry. They may not be a next-level leader for another ministry but for yours they are. One of the best short versions of what a next-level leader looks like for you is that they meet your qualifications in four areas: character, competence, chemistry, and culture. Let me, in this next section, go over ways to examine potential candidates in these four crucial areas.

Character: Ten Commandments - He plays by the rules: God's, Country's, Church's

The person who is a great hire has moral boundaries. You do not need to worry about them going off and doing something shady. I call that living inside the Ten box. This means that they stay within the boundaries of the Ten Commandments. Let's take a look at the basics here:

No other gods before me: They clearly put God first, not sports, fame, money, etc. They have an active relationship with God that is positive and obvious.

No idols: They have an accurate understanding of God. They know enough about God that they will be able to accurately teach and discuss who He is. They are not blending Christianity with other ideas or systems.

No cursing or swearing: They have their tongue under control. They do not swear or curse. They give a positive representation of the gospel in how they live, work, and play.

Remember the Sabbath Day: They worship God every day. They and their family make church a priority in their time. This person takes time off and knows how to enjoy life outside of work. They are not a workaholic.

Honor your father and mother: They know how to live under authority. They are respectful of authorities. They are not a rebel.

No murder: They are not violent or threatening. They do not lead or get their way through violence, the threat of violence, or the power of their personality. They do not devalue people or specific groups of people. They use the power of persuasion and logic, not position and threats. They are open to new ideas and real debate over issues.

No adultery: They are sexually faithful to their spouse and to God. Their lusts are under control. They are not involved with pornography or sensual pursuits.

No stealing: They are honest. They have no history of stealing, cheating, or cutting legal or moral corners. This person knows the rules in their ministry, state, and country and abides by them.

No lying: They are honest. They are not deceptive. What they say is the truth without shades of gray mixed in. They are not manipulative. Reports from them are full and trustworthy.

No coveting of other people's things: They are not schemers. They are not dreamers without plans. They are not filled with envy and jealousy. They can celebrate other people's success.

Sometimes it is very helpful to ask people who know this candidate to evaluate them on these ten different scales. Ask references and people who know them to rate their actual practice on a scale of one to ten in each of these ten areas. One is negative and ten is positive.

Competence: Evangelism, Discipleship, Worship, Fellowship, Compassion, Servant/Leaders

The church is the hope of the world, but unfortunately many churches and ministries have settled for incompetent people heading up crucial ministries. One of my pet peeves is that ministry leaders and boards are often unwilling to go after the highest capacity leaders or unwilling to let go of a good person who gets nothing done. We settle for a level of mediocrity that is killing the impact of the church. Jesus deserves the best we can give Him and His program deserves the best leadership we can find. Ministries, at times, excuse their lack of progress for all kinds of "spiritual" reasons. I am not suggesting that we treat ministers like assembly line workers; but I am advocating that we ask a pastor and/or ministry staff person to produce the appropriate people, programs, volunteers, leaders, prayers, or whatever. They should be willing to be held accountable for producing those numbers. They should be rewarded for meeting them, helped through training if they are not, or released if they cannot meet them.

It must be clear that any potential ministry hire understands how to deliver results in the six crucial areas of ministry: Evangelism, Discipleship, Worship, Fellowship, Compassion, Servant/Leaders. If there is no track record or talent for accomplishing these six things, then the person is most likely not a next-level hire. Some departments may require more of one of the major six than another, but these six are what ministry is all about.

Ô **Evangelism**: Do people become Christians under their ministry and leadership?.

Ô **Discipleship**: Do people grow in their ability to live as a follower of Christ under their ministry and leadership?

Ô **Worship**: Are people drawn to exalt and magnify God under their ministry and leadership?

Ô **Fellowship**: Do people form tight friendships and spiritual bonds under their ministry and leadership?

Ô **Compassion**: Are people taught to express love for the poor, afflicted, oppressed, and vulnerable under their ministry and leadership?

Ô **Servants and Leaders**: Are people drawn to serve and develop into leaders under this person's ministry and leadership?

Since these six things are what ministry is, then a person who is being asked to build a ministry must be able to do these. Look for these basic competencies and then whatever other competencies that are needed.

Another way to evaluate people in the leadership/ competence arena is to evaluate their basic personality and work orientation. I have found the system that Jack Welch used in working with people is very helpful in helping evaluate next-level leaders. He used the 4E – 1P grid. This stands for Energy, Energize, Edge, Execution, and Passion. These five qualities or expressions were always at the heart of a high quality, high capacity person who could lead significant initiatives. They often had to be trained and given experience, but this grid helped make a more accurate assessment on who would be the best leaders long term. Rate the potential candidates in these five areas on a sliding scale of 1 – 10 or as Welch did by filling in a circle ¼, ½, ¾, or fully.

Let's go through these in a little more detail. For much more detail on this system look at Jack and Suzy Welch's book, *Winning*.

Energy: These people are just full of life with excess energy and a desire to work hard and long. They are not dragging themselves through the day but have a tireless work ethic and energy. These people usually enjoy work and free time.

Energize: These people have the ability to energize others. People want to work for them and with them. People around them work harder, longer, and with more enthusiasm. It is easy to work with these people because of the energy in the place. There are some people who just drain the room of its energy by the way they act, speak, or work.

Edge: This is the person who can make the tough calls. They can make decisions without all the facts and be right much of the time. They are decisive. They are not hasty, but they make decisions and move on. These people do not stall, review, or study an item to death.

Execution: These are the people who get things done. They meet their numbers and good things happen in their area. Things change when they are around. They make things happen and it is usually the right things.

Passion: They have a real passion for their area of ministry whether it is children's, worship, preaching, adults, students, or whatever. It is clear that they are passionate about what they are doing and it keeps them at it. They do not become jaded and/or cynical about ministry, people, or the church.

Let me add a somewhat controversial element for ministry competence: the numbers. In Exodus 18, as we saw earlier, Jethro tells Moses that there are ten-level leaders, fifty-level leaders, hundred-level leaders, and thousand-level leaders. These numbers are fairly accurate barometers of the ability of a leader to attract, hold, and direct a certain number of people. Some people excel at attracting and leading ten people. They usually major on shepherding and care. They personally invest in the people under their charge. They make great small group leaders and Sunday school teachers. Some leaders are good at organizing fifty plus people. Usually the leader of fifty is an organizer, and their leadership ability is organizing the chaos that is already happening. These are usually the department heads in a medium-sized church: Sunday School Superintendent; Junior High Director; Women's Ministry Director; etc. Some leaders are able to attract, hold, and direct about a hundred people or more. These people often are powerful personalities or nonstop workers. The singular aspect of this type of leader is that they usually have to be in the center of all the action. When you ask a hundred-level leader to make the Worship Department significantly improve, they think to themselves, "What do I have to do to make this go forward?" Now this is in contradistinction to the thousand-level leader who says to himself, "Who can I get to take that ministry area to the next level?" The thousand-level leader is about planning, direction, recruiting, and decisions. They know that they can never build a team or organization of a thousand without strong leaders around them. My observation about these different level leaders is that ten-level leaders and fifty-level leaders usually produce health in an organization and not growth. On the other hand one hundred-level leaders and thousand-level leaders produce growth. A church needs both; but if you are looking for this next hire to really help the church grow, then you are looking for a person who has demonstrated an ability to gather a hundred or more people around them. I have watched pastors put ten-level and fifty-level leaders into prominent positions of leadership because they took direction well. Then usually a year or so later they are deeply frustrated that no growth has taken place. Therefore one of the questions that every pastor and Christian leader must answer is what level leader is this person I am thinking about hiring? What in their personality, past, talent, or gifting suggests their level of numerical leadership?

There are a number of other assessment tools that help in sorting out the kind of worker and leader a person will be: The DISC test, the Myers Briggs Type Indicator, The Strengths Finders, and many others.

Chemistry: Fruit of the Spirit – Are they enjoyable to be around and work with

It is crucial for any new hire to be able to get along with the other people on staff and in the office. They must have good chemistry with the people above them and below them as well as colleagues. Few things are more difficult than to have a sour, cynical person in the office bringing everyone down with them. We spend too much time at work to be with people who are not enjoyable to be with. This issue of chemistry is often overlooked, but it is crucial to a cohesive team. I tend to evaluate people on the chemistry issue over the fruit of the spirit. Do they allow the evidence of the Holy Spirit flowing through their life?

Love: Do they meet needs in others? Do they pursue the soul of others through listening and sharing? Do they do the little things to please people? Are they self-focused?

Joy: Do they have a positive focus? Do they develop deep relationships? Do they enjoy life both at work and outside work? Are they overly cynical and negative?

Peace: Do they have the ability to stop fighting even if they haven't won? Do they know how to make peace with someone they disagree with? Can they harmonize with another person's melody? Do they seem to have a lot of disagreements and people problems?

Patience: Can they wait and keep working for positive results? Can they persevere without lots of positive results? Are they impatient?

Kindness: Are they pleasantly helpful? Are they pleasant even when things are not going their way? Do they always seem put out by helping?

Goodness: Are they beneficial to others? Do they do the righteous thing? Do they benefit others when there is no reward for themselves?

Meekness: Are they flexible and adaptable? Are they angry? Can they apologize to others?

Faithfulness: Do they persevere in the face of opposition? Can they set a goal and continue pushing towards it over a long time? Are they impulsive and faddish?

Self-Control: Are they excessive in anything? Are they moderate in all things? Are there any obvious areas of excess?

Culture: Philosophy – They share the church's style and agenda

Every church and every ministry leader has a philosophy of ministry. It is best when these match so that the individual and the church are not pulling in different directions. I have found that it is possible to understand a church's and an individual's philosophy of ministry by asking them which two of the five purposes they prefer over the other three. The five main purposes of the church are Evangelism, Discipleship, Worship, Compassion, and Fellowship. All churches have to do all five purposes, but most churches prefer two of the five. Some churches are Discipleship and Evangelism churches. Some churches are Evangelism and Worship Churches. Some churches are Discipleship and Fellowship churches. Some churches are Fellowship and

Compassion churches. This offers a quick-look philosophy of ministry. Each candidate also tends to prefer two of the five purposes above the other three. It is best if the candidate matches the philosophy of ministry of the church. The obvious exception to this is if they are being asked to head up a specialized department: i.e., Worship, Evangelism, Compassion. In those cases they need to have that department objective in their preference and philosophy. But the second preference that they have should match one of the church's preferences.

I have also found that there are socio-economic and cultural fits between churches and their candidates. It is best to match the socio-economic background of a candidate with a church of a similar level. It usually will not work to have a bowling pastor in a tennis playing church. I have watched larger churches that have been in a middle-class area attract staff from an upper-class church. While doing ministry is the same, many of the assumptions are different and it can cause problems.

Another philosophy or cultural fit is generational. Every twenty-year period tends to see the emphasis and style of ministry differently. The younger person in ministry sees ministry differently than the middle-aged person. The person who is sixty-plus tends to see ministry differently than middle-aged minister. Generational differences should not be ignored but instead understood and utilized. If a church is completely one-generational in its approach, it can add other generations slowly and only after lots of discussion.

There are lots of different types and styles of church from theological to seeker, from traditional to Pentecostal. These different styles represent a way of doing ministry that will not usually mesh well with a different style. I have seen a number of problems develop when a person from a different style of church is recruited. The assumptions are all wrong. Usually the new staff member is being asked to fill in a weakness in the church. But they are asked to fix that weakness using the ministry assumptions and resources of the current church's style. This usually causes problems with funding, reporting, boundaries, results, etc. These kinds of problems can be overcome with lots of communication and clear expectations.

Step #4   Hire a next-level leader and let them do their thing

There are two potential problems that are fixed by this step. First, the church will not be willing to actually pull the trigger on one of the candidates, letting the others go to other ministries. Second, once the next-level leader is hired, they are given as much room as possible to implement their system and produce results.

It is essential that after you have thoroughly evaluated the appropriate next-level leader that you choose one of them. I have watched churches fumble the ball at this point. They have two or three excellent candidates, and they cannot decide which one to hire because there are good points about all of them. Some churches and pastors become unable to make a decision because they like all the candidates. If you wait too long, the choice will be made for you and usually you will get the lesser of the candidates.

A second problem that happens in some churches is that they will take a bright, creative leader and cram them into their old program structure. This inevitably de-motivates the leader and causes them to start sending out resumes for a church that will let them do ministry their way. Too often the Senior Pastor has a very detailed way to do a particular ministry that they know will work if a bright and energetic person were just to follow their prescription. Very few next-level leaders are excited about wearing Saul's armor into battle. They want to be considered an expert in their field. They want to be given every opportunity to design their own program. They want as much room as possible to make ministry happen.

The wise leader hires next-level leaders and gives them broad objectives then releases them to produce those results their way. There needs to be accountability and performance reviews, but next-level leaders want to be evaluated putting their ideas into practice. If they are to be fired for not accomplishing the appropriate level of leadership, they want to have put their blood, sweat, and tears into their way of doing it. If the leader "knows" that the new leader's ways will absolutely not work, then they should not be hired. They should not be hired with the idea of cramming them into someone else's system.

Conclusion

Remember, organizing the chaos that you already have is not the next level – whether a church is recruiting a volunteer leader or hiring a new department head. Too many churches make the mistake of hiring someone to organize or improve a ministry that is already functioning in the church. When a person is recruited or hired, the pastor, board, and other leaders need to be confident that this person will take the new ministry to the next level. There needs to be more visitor flow to your services; more people coming to faith in Christ; more people acting biblically in the arenas of their life; more people worshipping God; more people connecting deeply to others; more people sharing the love of Christ with the poor, afflicted and oppressed; more people serving; and finally more leaders.

LEADERSHIP SKILL #4 - LEADERSHIP DEVELOPMENT
Developing yourself, current leaders, and new leaders

What if your church had an abundance of godly leaders? What if your ministry had a proven process for developing godly leaders and that every year produced new leaders that could take on important kingdom projects? What if the current leaders in the church felt a constant sense of encouragement and growth that made them fulfilled and happy to be investing in your church? This chapter is designed to help you produce that kind of church.

Years ago, when I first started as a young pastor, I quickly became frustrated by the lack of leadership in the church I was serving. It seemed like I had to do everything. I became a pastor to change the world and yet my church didn't have enough leaders to change children's ministry, let alone the community. I realized I had a huge problem. As a pastor I had all kinds of dreams and goals for the church and the community. My problem was that we did not have enough leaders to cover the few things we were already doing, let alone all the new dreams. Also, the men and women with the highest leadership potential in my church were not volunteering. Most of them were so busy that they did well to attend three Sunday services a month. Their work, their family, and the community were all clamoring for more of them; and they did not have time for extra meetings or Bible studies during the evenings. I decided to go back to a strategy

I had used effectively when I was a youth pastor: invite each high-potential leader who was in any way connected to the church to a lunch where I challenged them to set aside one lunch per week to be involved in a spiritual-growth action group I was forming. This was not a Bible study but was going to be action-oriented with new spiritual exercises every week. This was going to be high-level spiritual training.

It worked. Every August I would prayerfully construct a list of high-potential but uninvolved leaders that I knew (some did not even attend our church). As I stated earlier, I would ask each of them to come to a lunch where I would ask them point blank if they were interested in growing spiritually. If they were ready to be challenged spiritually, I invited them to a weekly lunch, near their place of business with other high-potential leaders. The groups were never bigger than five including myself. This was not a Bible Study but rather an action group where every week I would show them a spiritual exercise and then ask them to do it the next week. Each week we would spend the first half hour hearing how last week's exercise worked out when they did it. If they did not do the exercise, then we would repeat the same exercise during the present week. I guaranteed them that they would be different people in a few short months if they jumped in. This was a challenge and usually two-thirds of the people that I invited jumped in. Every year I would mentor and disciple sixteen to twenty high-potential, uninvolved leaders in our church. At the end of nine to twelve months I would ask them where they would like to serve in the church, and they always started serving with gusto. Every year our church added great people engaging their leadership talents for the Lord. This idea caught on and our lay elders started doing the same thing with people in the church and people at their work. I required the ministerial staff to do this with at least six people every year. Through this process we saw a continual stream of new leaders entering ministry at our church. Some staff developed their high-potential folks completely different from the process that I used.

Whatever method, books, or system they used it could not be a Bible study; but it must be action or application driven. It must actually cause changes in a high-potential leader's life. It must make them godly. Usually I suggested to staff that whatever caused them to grow into a godly person is what they should make these folks go through.

Every year our church saw twenty to forty new leaders volunteer to help the mission and vision of the church because we had spent the previous year pouring ourselves into helping those leaders become functioning godly leaders. When they had practically seen the power of Christ change their marriages, themselves, their families, and their work, they were ready to release some of their leadership energy to help the church.

Leadership development is one of the greatest needs in every ministry. And yet there is very little focus on this problem in most churches. There are three major problems in the area of leadership development. First, the individual leader must keep growing every year. If not, then he/she will continue to advocate what has already been advocated only with increasing effort and shrillness. The leader must clearly be seen as learning, growing, developing, and changing or people will lose confidence in their leadership. Second, the current leaders in the ministry must be developed and resourced every year. If not, then burn-out sets in. There is an epidemic of burned out church staff who gave their best to a church only to be used, abused, and cast aside when they wore out. Third, new leaders must be raised up every year to meet the ever growing demands of ministry. Ministry cannot grow without an expanding base of leaders. This chapter is designed to practically address these challenges.

I will talk about these three crucial leadership development issues in reverse order of their importance. I will discuss raising up new leaders first. I will talk about developing the current leaders second. I will explore growing personally as a leader in the final section of this chapter.

Raising Up New Leaders

There is a screaming need in every church for more leaders. NO ministry has too many leaders. Yet most ministries do not have a realistic plan that will produce new leaders every year. Almost every ministry waits for leaders to come prepackaged to them from somewhere else. Therefore the skilled leader sets up a system or systems in which new leaders are produced every year.

My experience is that the highest potential leaders in your church will not come to the programmatic education system of your church. This is very frustrating to most pastors. The best people don't attend the classes and groups you put together. They are too busy and that approach is not intimate, fast, or active enough to capture high-level leaders. Many of these people have used their leadership in business, politics, education, and other arenas. They have had significant levels of success, but they do not really comprehend or practice their Christianity. They would be willing to engage in growing as a Christian if it was taught by someone they respected and not in the classroom model. They want to be mentored, coached, and/or trained; not instructed.

In most cases leadership development in a church is not about leadership at all; it is about development of dynamic Christianity in people who are already leaders. Christian leaders are people who actually practice their Christianity and have leadership skills and gifting. Therefore Christian leadership development begins with active discipleship to those with leadership gifts. After a person is truly practicing their faith then their natural leadership can be harnessed, refined, and expanded.

Frank was a hugely successful businessman who occasionally attended our church but was not involved. Men like him, who have incredibly high leadership potential, should be recruited into a full orbed practice of Christianity and the work of God. He accepted the challenge to meet with me over lunch once a week with other business leaders to grow spiritually. He began a journey into spiritual depth and power that continues dynamically to this day. God used the action group he joined to inject him with a virulent dose of Christianity and he has never recovered. Dozens and dozens of men and women just like him have been enflamed with the cause of Christ through these small mentoring action groups.

There are many different ways and/or systems to raise up new leaders for Christ's kingdom. I have run across a few that have been quite effective. I am sure that there are many others that I have not yet heard of that also produce mature godly Christian leaders. Whatever system you use, it must actually produce increasing numbers of mature, godly leaders or it is not a good system. Exchanging biblical content from one notebook to another notebook is not leadership development. The system you use must bring about changed actions in a leader.

John Maxwell used a system that he called prayer partners in which he developed people into mature Christians through once-a-month prayer breakfasts. He taught them everything that they needed to know through the vehicle of prayer. This is an active and intimate method that has worked for many. I would recommend that you look at John Maxwell's excellent resource, *The Pastor's Prayer Partners*.

I utilized a form of small groups that I call "action groups." Every year during August I would begin making a list of high-potential leaders who might be invited to one of the action groups around the city. A great amount of prayer went into the list and invitations. Every year about a third of the list would decline to be included for various reasons, but I usually ended up with sixteen to twenty who were ready to go for broke in learning how to live their Christianity.

These groups were three or four committed leaders meeting for an hour over lunch to learn a new spiritual exercise. The first half hour was spent hearing about what happened when each person tried last week's exercise. The next ten minutes of the lunch was hearing about the new exercise. In five to ten minutes I would describe and demonstrate the spiritual exercise I wanted the leaders to try during the next week. Each of them had books and resources which explained the exercise in more detail. They could read these during the week. I was not studying a passage or explaining the exercise in detail. I was showing them how to do it, so they could actually do it. If anyone had a question about how to do it or why it was important, they could ask during that five to ten minutes. The final part of our lunch together involved taking prayer requests from each person. Prayer requests gave people the opportunity to unzip a little bit of their soul to the others each week. This allowed the group to bond and care for one another. Growth came through the connections that were built between leaders and through the changes brought on by the exercises.

I have recently found that I can use the action group format in larger settings if the larger group is broken into smaller groups of three or four. It is the smaller group that listens to the actual application of the exercises. It is the smaller group that listens to prayer requests and prays together. The actual explanation of the exercises is still only ten minutes – maybe a little longer – with the bulk of the time spent in talking and listening in the small groups. I still believe that it is the tight knit smaller group that carries the load of the life change, but it is possible to gather lots of small groups into once-a-week gatherings and process through these crucial issues and exercises together.

I found that a particular order of the exercises was most helpful. We would take about four months trying and practicing spiritual disciplines to improve their direct connection to God. This usually lasted from September through December. Starting in January we went for three months, improving their marriage through marital exercises. This usually lasted January through March. The next section of exercises dealt with conquering anger, lust, and our tongue. This lasted as long as the leaders needed to work in these areas. Remember each meeting was about the exercises and applying the biblical material. The meetings were not teaching times or studies. It was about the leaders talking about what happened when they tried the exercise and what was happening in their lives. Following that section on anger, lust, and tongue control, we would move on to time management and then financial management. This process would take nine months to a year and would bring significant changes to the leaders involved. Once the foundations of an active Christian life were embedded underneath their leadership skills and gifts, then their God-given calling could take over. I would also feed the groups tapes that discussed doctrine and theology so that their understanding of a biblical worldview was also growing.

This process became so significant for our church that the church board asked me to focus my attention as Senior Pastor on doing two things: preaching on Sundays and raising up new leaders through my small action groups. Every year the staff members of our church would release dozens of leaders into the various ministries in our church and into the community.

Let me explain that I did not concentrate on their doctrinal or theological understanding until after they were making significant strides in their application of biblical principles. I believe that the Apostle Peter set the pattern for faith's development when he stated that after faith, it was virtue that was needed and then after virtue, knowledge could and should be developed (2 Peter 1:5-8). It has been my experience if a person adds too much doctrine and/ or theological development before they learn to love, give, and express Christ's joy, they can become proud Pharisees in their knowledge. After a person is living out their faith\, then doctrinal and theological truth is very helpful.

This leadership development process proved so successful for our church that I began requiring every full-time ministerial staff person to personally mentor six to ten high-potential men, if they were men, and high-potential women, if they were women. We followed the principle that it was best for women to develop women and men to develop men so that temptation would be reduced and intimate matters could be discussed with a higher level of bluntness. Those recruited were to be people who were not currently involved in their ministry but high-potential leaders that they knew in the church or in the community. Each staff person would mentor or coach in their own way. But the key metric was whether their way produced ten new leaders in their ministry area every two years. If it did, then wonderful; if it didn't, then they needed to change what they were doing or we would have to change them.

Let me sum up how radically important it is to raise up new leaders. I have been involved in helping all kinds of churches get healthy and grow for over twenty years now. The only common element that causes growth is more leaders. This is the controlling insight for health and growth – more leaders. The church that has an increasing number of leaders helping it do ministry will almost always be growing. Let me state the obvious corollaries: the ministry that has the same number of leaders will be stagnant; the ministry that has a declining number of leaders will shrink. In order to have a growing, healthy ministry there must be more godly leaders this year than there was last year. The group of churches that I have served in have grown in average attendance from 4,200 to over 12,300 in five years by raising up more leaders in their ministries. The pastors are growing as leaders, but the key is that they have more leaders helping them. Raise up more leaders and the ministry will be able to expand. We cannot get the job of worldwide Christian expansion done without more leaders. Some ministries believe that the only way to do this is by hiring more leaders. This is not a bad way if you have the resources, but it often leaves the huge mass of potential leaders untapped. Find a way to develop them and you will have an almost inexhaustible supply of new leaders.

Current Leadership Development

There is a second arena of leadership development that is often going unnoticed. It is the problem of current leaders – both vocational and volunteer – feeling used, burned out, uncared for, and undeveloped. Many people come on staff at a church thinking it will be the best place to work with the most love and personal growth that they have ever experienced and just the opposite takes place. There is an epidemic of burned-out church staff and lay volunteers in Christian ministry these days. I regularly hear staff and lay leaders say things like, "I used to have time to love God until I came on staff at this church." "My family life has really suffered ever since I took this ministry position." "I am exhausted and do not think that I can continue to run at this pace – I may have to quit ministry to get my life back." It is becoming so prevalent that web sites start up like the one called "Death by Ministry." This website lists the following frightening statistics.

The following statistics were presented by Pastor Darrin Patrick from such organizations as Barna Research Organization and Focus on the Family:

- Ô Fifteen-hundred pastors leave the ministry each month due to moral failure, spiritual burnout, or contention in their churches. Fifty percent of pastors' marriages will end in divorce.
- Ô Eighty percent of pastors and eighty-four percent of their spouses feel unqualified and discouraged in their role as pastors.
- Ô Fifty percent of pastors are so discouraged that they would leave the ministry if they could but have no other way of making a living.
- Ô Eighty percent of seminary and Bible school graduates who enter the ministry will leave the ministry within the first five years.

Ô Seventy percent of pastors constantly fight depression.

Ô Eighty percent of pastors' spouses feel their spouse is overworked.

Ô Eighty percent of pastors' spouses wish their spouse would choose another profession.

Ô The majority of pastors' wives surveyed said that the most destructive event that has occurred in their marriage and family was the day they entered the ministry. (Death by Ministry website: http://mrclm.blogspot.com/2006/06/death-by-ministry-burnout.html)

There is a deadly assumption in Christian ministry that leads to the high level of ministry burn-out that currently takes place. The assumption is that people who become pastors, ministers, or even lay volunteer leaders do not need any encouragement, care, or leadership development; they have it all together. This false assumption is what causes most ministries to give no thought to developing, ministering, and encouraging the current leaders in the ministry. This always leads to using people's time, energy, and resources and then discarding them when they can't keep up. The church must recognize that the people who have signed on to help the church move forward also have needs and that a fair bit of training and encouragement must be directed towards them.

This means that each week – and at a minimum each month – these people who are serving and leading ministry need more than just the Sunday message and their small group. They need leadership ideas, deeper theological understanding, and inspiration. They need mentoring, caring, direction, and listening. How can you accomplish all this? There are probably a number of different ways of doing this, but let me suggest one way. Each full-time vocational leader of a ministry should have a thirty-to-sixty minute one-on-one personal meeting with their direct report once a week or once every other week. This meeting would be divided into two parts: the first half to hear about progress in their role, issues, problems, ideas, and needed resources; the second half to hear about how the person is doing in their life – interacting at the level that the staff person wants to share. Great leaders must care about their people. This means that they must know about their life outside of work. I believe that everyone has ten major relationships in life and the health of those relationships define your life. The ten major relationships are: God, Self, Marriage/Dating, Family, Work, Church, Friends, Money, Society, Enemies. Great leaders know what is happening in these arenas in their people's lives.

In addition to the one-on-one meeting once a week, all staff should be invited to a meeting for new ideas, training in theology, fun, and inspiration. I have found most people in ministry constantly need new ideas, fresh understanding, and development in four kinds of leadership: Relational Leadership; Doctrinal Leadership; Organizational Leadership; Leadership Skills. The following chart will show you the four areas with the sub-categories that all staff need constant training and new information about. I constantly look over this list and ask myself what the staff needs at that time in their development. They need to know that you care about their growing and not just the work they do. The following chart has the four types of leadership arranged in four columns, but there is no correlation between the columns. These are just four lists of ten elements in leadership.

Relational Leadership	Doctrinal Leadership	Organizational Leadership	Leadership Skills
God	Bible	Leadership	Reality
Self	God	Equipping	Vision
Marriage/ Dating	Jesus	Assimilation	Change
Family	Holy Spirit	Discipleship	Wisdom
Work	Man	Evangelism	People Skills
Church	Salvation Sin	Resources	Self-Discipline
Money	Church	Spiritual	Systematize Delegate
Society	Angels	Heart	Raising Resources
Friends	Heaven, Hell, Judgment Day	Organization	Next-Level People
Enemies	Last Things	Purpose	Development

I have listed the top ten areas under each of these headings. As I look at this chart, I pray for the staff and volunteers and ask which of these above areas do my people need more training, information, or inspiration about. Every week I want to bring one, two, or three ideas, exercises, or truths that will help the people on staff to move forward personally or professionally. My goal in working with staff and lay volunteers has been for them to say, "I haven't always agreed with everything the church or Gil did, but I grew more and was challenged the most under his ministry." There are a number of ways of using the above topics and ideas. Sometimes I would give multiple topics to hit a wider swath of ministry people. Sometimes I would drill into one topic for a few weeks because everybody needed to get this. Sometimes I might do a book review that gets at one of the topics. Sometimes I might bring in an expert from the seminary, business, or education to help us see or grasp this issue. Sometimes we would watch a video about one of these issues or read a book together. Sometimes I might have a staff person present the material. Sometimes we may need to go to a conference to add a particular growth element. What must be clear is that the church cares for its staff and wants them to grow to their maximal potential.

Significant time, energy, and resources must be given to the current leaders who are allowing the ministry to continue. They must know that you care for them. They must know that you want their best even if it conflicts with your goals. They must know that they will be stretched, developed, and grown as long as they serve in this ministry. They must feel that you will plan with them, work with them, and celebrate with them; not just drive them. The church must become a great place to work where the highest standards of integrity and care are lavished upon those who work there.

Personal Development

A third area of needed leadership development is for each leader to continually keep growing as a person and as a leader. If any leader stops growing, the results will eventually become evident. Let me give you a couple of examples. Pastor Dan stopped growing the day he finished seminary. He believed that he knew everything about church and how to do it effectively. Pastor Dan was a wonderful pastor who went to seminary when the ideal size of a ministry was two hundred fifty. His gifting, abilities, and personable manner would have allowed him to lead a church over a thousand, but he kept sabotaging his church's growth with his stagnant body of knowledge. He continued reverting back to all the things that he learned in seminary. Everyone who heard him preach commented on how he should be preaching to hundreds more each week; but no matter what he did, his church would not grow past two hundred fifty. Because he did not go to seminars or read church organization books, his mind was locked into a way of thinking which did not allow the church to expand. After thirty plus years in ministry and always being frustrated by his church's lack of continued growth, he left the ministry in defeat after a particularly disastrous series of leadership decisions. Every attempt to encourage him to grow was met with resistance or hostility. He already knew how to run the church. He already knew how to preach. He already knew what needed to happen in church. What more could these seminars, conferences, and retreats teach him? They could have taught him a lot if he had been open to learning. Someone once said, "Hardening of the viewpoint is more deadly than hardening of the arteries."

Let me tell you a success story about personal leadership development. Pastor Ron had never led a church over eighty in the twenty plus years of his ministry. He was open to learning and growing so that more could be impacted by Christ. I was able to introduce him to some new ideas and new concepts for impacting people with the gospel. He was the same guy with the same good news, but his ministry started to grow. He was amazed as his ministry began expanding until well over four hundred people attended every week. He confessed that he was regularly tempted to go back to doing ministry the way he had been doing it, but he knew that in a few short months his ministry would be eighty people again. He had grown and, therefore, his ministry could develop underneath him. His leadership abilities had been expanded, and he did not want to go back.

I meet pastors and ministry leaders who want their ministries to grow, but they don't perceive that they need to grow also. They want the new technique and the latest insight that when added to their ministry will cause it to double in size. The answer to their question is almost always that they need more leaders and that they need to grow as a leader personally. If they don't grow, it will be impossible for their ministry to have sustained growth.

There are far too many in ministry today who stopped growing when they finished seminary or after their first five years in ministry. When the leader is not growing, the organization will stagnate. An organization thrives on new ideas, new perspectives, and new methodologies. This requires that the leader meet new people, read new books, listen to different approaches. God is always raising up new people with new ideas to spread the gospel. As soon as a denomination or church thinks that they have THE way to do church, a new generation rises up who do not respond to that way. Because the church is constantly dealing with ancient manuscripts and long-standing traditions, the leadership of any church can get stagnant quickly.

Personal Leadership Development Plan

I regularly ask ministry leaders what is their personal leadership development plan. Do they have one? Are they following it? Unfortunately there is no requirement in most churches or denominations for the pastors or leaders to take courses, read books, or listen to new information. Many pastors only read books in a very narrow band which is not about growth but deeper information about what they already know. Church boards, denominations, and executive pastors should begin requiring that ministry leaders need continuing education units and/or some form of ministry development.

Every leader must have a personal leadership development plan. This can be complex or simple, but every leader needs one and needs to show that they are following it. I have talked to some ministry leaders who have very elaborate personal leadership development plans and some with very simple plans. The key is that you have a plan and you are growing as a leader because of that plan. Let me suggest a few basic plans.

The first and most obvious plan for many in ministry is to go back to school and get another degree or further education. For some this means getting a Bachelors degree or Masters degree or for others it means getting a Doctoral degree. For some who choose the formal education option as their leadership development plan, it does not matter if the education results in a degree; it only matters that they are challenged, stretched, and growing. If formal education is your leadership development plan, then continue taking classes. The range of ideas, professors, and new people will surely expand your leadership thinking. As a seminary professor I am aware of how powerful the undergraduate and graduate level is in stretching, growing, and developing people beyond their previous growth points. I know pastors who keep taking classes and keep piling up degrees because it helps them be on the cutting edge. Some pastors do not even take classes that have to do with the church or theology; they branch out into other areas of interest. Any type of growth is usually good and helpful.

My personal plan – while it has included a lot of formal education – follows the more practical and personal model. I try and read a book a week, listen to a few tapes or lectures per week, go to two conferences or retreats every year, study one outstanding leader each year (living or from the past), and make sure I meet new people and especially new leaders each year. Let me say that again in a little different way so you see it. I try to:

- Ô read a book a week
- Ô listen to a few tapes or lectures per week
- Ô go to two conferences or retreats every year
- Ô study one outstanding leader each year (living or from the past)
- Ô meet new people and especially new leaders each year

My ministry was completely turned around by attending seminars and conferences. I was exposed to thinking that I did not run across in seminary. I met people who challenged my thinking and encouraged my soul. Some of these people have become my closest friends. I learned how to solve numerous practical problems in the church through attending all different kinds of seminars and conferences. Not all of the conferences were life changing and impactful, but I usually grew in some way because of my attendance. I attended theology conferences, leadership conferences, small group conferences, church health conferences, spiritual formation conferences, pastors' conferences, and all kinds of other types of conferences. There has been incredible value in mining the practical insights of other leaders. Every new idea and new person that a leader interacts with pushes them to grow in some way. I heard a saying years ago that has stuck with me: "You will be exactly the same person you are today except for the books you read and people you meet." Pastors need to keep exposing themselves to new people and new aspects of God's knowledge.

There are hundreds of preprogrammed leadership and personal development plans like John Maxwell's 100 tapes on leadership; Oswald Sanders book, *Spiritual Leadership*; R.C. Sproul and John Gestener's tapes on *Systematic Theology*.; Benjamin Franklin's 13 different qualities (virtues) to be developed; Og Mandino's: *A Better Way to Live or The Greatest Salesman in the World.* I have encouraged different individuals to follow all or parts of these programs over the years. The list goes on and on; some of them are excellent and some are not helpful at all. The main ingredient in a successful program is that the leaders grow and be active with the information they are receiving. Information that is not acted upon or incorporated into ministry is usually quickly discarded.

When I started in ministry I was working off a whole backlog of information, ideas, and methods that worked well up to two hundred people. God was able to bless me through that information up to two hundred people, but my lack of information about how the church needed to be led beyond that number meant that I kept getting in the way. It was not until I started growing beyond the information that I received in seminary and started to learn how to lead a congregation beyond two hundred that the church was able to expand. It is not easy to admit that you are the bottleneck that keeps your ministry from growing. But it is often the reason. Embrace the idea that you will need to keep growing until Jesus calls you home. Talk with people who are being used by God successfully and see what they are doing that you are not. Learn to be very comfortable looking like the dumbest person in the room. Ask questions, allow yourself to be contradicted, explore completely new models, and do not allow yourself to believe you have it all settled in terms of methods.

Conclusion

The church rises or falls on the back of its leaders, PERIOD. The greatest gift a pastor can give the church is more leaders. One of the greatest gifts that a pastor can give himself is to keep growing as a leader. One of the most enduring gifts that a church can give to its staff and lay volunteers is continual leadership development wrapped in real love.

The gift of leadership development is so often overlooked and taken for granted, and yet it is the only common denominator in healthy, growing ministries worldwide. Spend the time to grapple with the different systems and put together a complete leadership development system – one for raising up new leaders, one for developing your current leaders, and one for developing yourself – and you will never be sorry. Life will become an adventure with new discoveries and new joys around each corner. Your perspectives and systems may look vastly different than the ones that I have outlined in this chapter, but if you raise up godly leaders then I applaud you. Keep going. What we must not do is go back to the "burb" method of leadership development where no one develops new leaders; where we just wait for one church to have a problem, "burb" out some of its leaders, and then we collect those damaged leaders and finish the process of using them up. Leaders are some of the most precious commodities in the church. Treasure them, grow them, find new ones, recruit them, raise them up; it will be worth it. A church that will focus its energy on raising up new leaders, and encouraging, and developing its current leaders, and make sure that EACH of its leaders keeps growing is unbeatable.

LEADERSHIP SKILL #5 - INITIATE AND MANAGE CHANGE

Churches must change or they will die. Change is a constant. Therefore developing skills for creating and handling change is required for leaders in the church. There are two major dangers when it comes to change that can destroy the church if not handled with skill. One is not starting enough change and the second is not managing the change process once it begins. Every church needs the right amount of change to constantly be injected into its ministry to be maximally effective.

Pastor Jim and the church were at a critical juncture. The church was averaging over two hundred people on a Sunday. Lots of new families were coming, offerings were over what the church needed to meet the budget. Pastor Jim was extremely busy but full of joy. He was single-handedly thrusting the church forward. The future looked bright as they stood at the crossroads of what to do next. Pastor Jim desperately needed staff and the money was coming in to begin funding several new staff positions. Certain key families seized control of the leadership and were advocating taking the surplus offerings and paying down the mortgage on the buildings.

Pastor Jim is a godly man who unhesitatingly gives of himself to solve the problems of the church and sacrificially cares for every member of his congregation, but he hates change and confrontation. His energy, skill, and sacrifice caused the church to grow. Unfortunately he did not have the leadership skills to initiate the correct changes or confront the key people at the critical moment and the opportunity was lost. If Pastor Jim had spoken up and agitated for the staff that he needed, the church would have responded positively, most likely grown, and saved Pastor Jim's health. But he was uncomfortable initiating change and disagreeing with powerful families in the church, so when the mortgage pay down idea started gaining steam, he went along. After all, they said, "Pastor Jim is doing just fine and isn't it biblical to pay down debt?" What Pastor Jim and those who were advocating for mortgage reduction didn't realize was that there were people in the church who needed staff to increase key programs so they wouldn't leave. Few also took into account that Pastor Jim could not continue working at his current pace indefinitely or he would jeopardize his health. So after a few years several key families could no longer wait for the youth and music ministry to improve and they began to leave in clumps – some very loudly. Pastor Jim took the bulk of the blame. Then in the midst of the crisis Pastor Jim's health began to fail and he could no longer run at a superhuman pace. All the while the church attendance slowly declined and paying off the mortgage became even a higher priority for certain members of the church. The mortgage was paid off ahead of schedule, but the ministry of the church and Pastor Jim were broken. The church lost over seventy-five percent of its attendance since its high water mark at that crucial leadership juncture and now has about fifty people attending. It will never recover under Pastor Jim's ministry and may not under any one. Pastor Jim needed to lead by initiating the search for new staff before the mortgage was paid off. In fact the mortgage may have needed to be reconfigured so that ministry could be increased. Now the building is paid for but few come to it.

A pastor must lead even if that's not his best skill or fits with his personality. There are times in the history of a ministry when initiating change is crucial and the point leader must act to initiate those changes. There will always be some opposition to change, even the great changes. Leaders must initiate anyway.

The other side of the change equation is illustrated by Pastor Greg. Pastor Greg believed if a program isn't working, then let's try something new; the cause of Christ is too important. For the first two years of his ministry every part of the church began growing. Pastor Greg's energy brought significant change without subtracting anything. After two years, however, there were changes that were needed. He didn't get approval to eliminate the stodgy youth program; he just made the changes and installed new youth leaders with new programs. He didn't have discussions with the choir director about quality or types of music or the need for a different kind of music. He just eliminated the choir music time from the service and asked people who could sing to begin singing special numbers. He didn't prepare the congregation with months of discussion and informative letters on how the congregational meetings would be different; he just didn't allow angry or belligerent individuals to talk in the meetings anymore.

As you can imagine, all kinds of people were offended. Pastor Greg's refusal to manage the change process plunged the congregation into years of problems and dysfunction. It took Pastor Greg nine years before he really understood the value and the how of managing the change process. This meant lots of wounds and scars that didn't have to happen if he had known how to manage the change process.

The Absolute Need for Change

Let's talk about why change is absolutely necessary for churches. In order to keep doing Evangelism, Discipleship, Worship, Compassion, and Fellowship effectively, change is required. In each of the five major purposes of the church the question must be asked, "What is the most effective way to accomplish this purpose?"

The answer will often mean change. Churches can easily become stagnant pools of the status quo where what worked in yesteryear is perpetuated even though it is no longer effective.

God and His eternal truths do not change and they must remain unaltered; but the way that ministry is delivered must change with different time periods, regional differences, cultural differences, etc. It is the wise church leaders who realize that we must be constantly ready to change to impact the world with the unchanging message of God's love.

Initiating Change: Doing and Asking

What are the basic ingredients to initiating change? There are two basic actions that initiate change: Doing and Asking. When a church is under two hundred people, the pastor's greatest weapon for change is his personal actions. In many cases the pastor is the only person who can act in a change-producing way. As a church gets larger there is less doing and more asking. This involves asking God in prayer, asking the staff, asking new members, asking the board, asking the congregation, etc. In order to exist and thrive above two hundred people, leadership must become very comfortable with asking the right people to do the right things at the right time. The leadership must constantly ask or very little that is significant will happen.

Biblical Examples

Do we have any biblical examples of initiating change through doing and asking? Yes, the obvious example is God himself. God acts. Through these actions He changes things. In these cases He does not act because He was asked but because it was a change that was needed. He decided to create the heavens and the earth and begin a search for worshippers who would worship

Him in spirit and truth. He decided to rain down plagues on the Egyptians to demonstrate His power. He decided to give Moses His laws and agreements for a just society. He sent His only begotten Son to rescue the world from it enslavement to sin. He decided to communicate through human writers His ideas and His words so that we would have a permanent record of the crucial information we need.

While God at times will act into our world, He often brings about change through asking someone to do something for Him. The list of biblical heroes is a list of men and women that God asked to get something started. Abraham was asked leave his home and head toward an unknown land and future. Moses was asked to confront the most powerful leader in the world. Joshua was asked to lead the people into the Promised Land and conquer the inhabitants who were already there. God asked Isaiah, "Whom shall I send?" "Who shall go for Us?" Jesus asked each of the apostles to follow Him. Jesus asked Saul of Tarsus "Why are you persecuting me?" and then asked him to be a worldwide traveler and promoter of Christianity as the true religion.

God is a change agent into this broken sinful world that has gone off the course He originally set for it. He acts into the flow of history and He asks people to do specific missions for Him. We can and should follow His pattern in bringing about positive and righteous change. There is change that is needed all around us and we must act and ask to make it happen.

Basic Questions for Initiating Change through Doing

The following are a list of some of the questions that will help you think through the actions that you could take that would begin the change process that is needed in your ministry. For those of you who do not initiate easily, these questions may be crucial to crystallizing your leadership. For those of you who initiate easily, these questions may become a launching pad to far more significant questions and actions.

Ô   What are the actions that you can take that would bring about the positive change God is after? Make a list.

Ô   What needs to be done but no one wants to do it? Make a list.

Ô   What three things could be done that would immediately be noticed as positive?

Ô   What could be left undone and very few would notice?

Ô   What are you currently doing every week? Following the 20/80 rule: What are the top 20% of your actions that make the most difference? What are the 80% of your actions that produce little or no action?

Ô   What action could you take that would make a 50% difference in Evangelism this year?

Ô   What action could you take that would make a 50% difference in Discipleship this year?

Ô   What action could you take that would make a 50% difference in Worship this year?

Ô   What action could you take that would make a 50% difference in Fellowship this year?

Ô   What action could you take that would make a 50% difference in Compassion this year?

Basic Questions for Initiating Change through Asking

The following are a list of some of the questions that will help you think through the questions that you could ask that would begin the change process that is needed in your ministry. For those of you who do not initiate easily, these questions may be crucial to crystallizing your leadership. For those of you who initiate easily, these questions may become a launching pad to far more significant questions and actions.

- Ô What can you give away that you are currently doing?
- Ô What should the future of your ministry look like in three to five years?
- Ô Who could be asked to start the new initiative?
- Ô What needs to be asked to make a 50% difference in the next year?
- Ô What hard questions are being avoided?
- Ô Who needs to be held accountable for the lack of positive direction?
- Ô Who has the skills to move the church forward in the critical area?
- Ô What amount of money is needed to accomplish the crucial goals?
- Ô Who could give that money?
- Ô How could we raise that money?
- Ô Who needs to be involved with our evangelism efforts who is not involved now, if it is to be improved by 100% this year?
- Ô Who needs to be involved in our helping people mature in Christ, who is not involved now, if we are to become 100% more effective by this time next year?
- Ô Who needs to be a part of worship who is not involved now, if it is to improve by 100% this year?
- Ô Who needs to be a part of compassion ministries who is not involved now, if it is to improve by 100% this year?
- Ô Who needs to be a part of fellowship efforts who is not involved now, if it is to be improved by 100% this year?

Managing Change: Communication and Personalities

Communication

What are the basic ingredients to managing change? There are two basic issues in working through a change process that will always come up: communication and personalities. The more communication that precedes, accompanies, and celebrates change, the better the process will go. Different people react to change and conflict differently and understanding these differences can allow a much more positive change process.

Communication is the overarching key action for the change process. There are a multitude of means of communicating. Making sure that there are abundant and redundant forms of communication is essential to a healthy change process. It seems most helpful to break down a change process into three basic components and look at the amount of communication needed in each part. The first part of any change process is that which precedes the actual change process. Communication in this part involves discussions, brainstorming, planning, coordinating, approvals, prayer, etc. The basic skill here is that everyone who needs to know and contribute in this change is brought into the loop in the appropriate way. The smaller the organization, the less people need to be involved in this pre-change communication process.

The second part of any change process is once the change is being implemented or pursued. Communication in this part involves: announcements, progress reports, meetings, mid-course corrections, suggestions, prayer, constant repetition of the goal, raising funds, and resources, etc. The most destructive thing at this point in the change process is silence and a belief that this process is on auto-pilot. Any change process can veer off course, crash, be hijacked, or die from lack of support if the communication among participants is not kept up. This is a skill that can be learned so that there is less collateral damage in a change process.

The third part of the change process is that which takes place after the change has been accomplished. Many wonderful changes, even after they have been implemented, have failed to produce the long-term results that were envisioned because this third part of the process had a communication breakdown. After a change takes place, the communication element involves: celebrations, thank-yous, plaques, pictures, newspaper articles, announcements, rewards, gifts, etc. Unfortunately many churches ignore the need for these final forms of communication, and so the change is not fully enjoyed and the next change is more difficult to attempt.

Personalities

The second crucial issue in managing change is understanding the different reactions of people to change and conflict. Whole books, courses, seminars, and programs have been constructed to develop the needed skills in this area. While much of what has been discovered in this area is helpful, the two most basic understandings will go a long way to navigating through the minefield of people's different reactions. First, mentally put people in your organization on a continuum in terms of their adoption of new ideas and programs. This continuum usually looks something like this:

Early Adopters –

Middle Adopters –

Late Adopters –

Never Adopters

Early Adopters are people who are always excited about a new idea or a new program. These are the people who need to be enlisted at the beginning. **Middle Adopters** are people who do not immediately like every idea or program, but they are not too difficult to persuade if you can get it started or a prototype constructed. Next are **Late Adopters** who resist change for a long time and must see a long track record of positive results before they will embrace something new. By the time this group starts embracing something, it is no longer a new idea. It would be ridiculous to try and get approvals from this group for new ideas unless lots of other organizations have already had a long track record of success. Finally there are a group of **Never Adopters** who will never adopt a new idea. They are still typing on a typewriter, calling on a land line, etc. If it has *new* attached to it, they will never be for the concept. With these four different approaches to new ideas you need to approach different people at different times through the change process. Do not ask a Late or Never Adopter to get on board with a new idea. It just will not happen. Instead, approach Early Adopters and get the momentum built through their enthusiasm and expertise. If lots of changes are going to be needed in your organization, start putting Early and Middle Adopters in the key leadership positions so that change is possible.

Another essential people understanding that has proven very helpful in working through change and conflict is Norman Shawchuck's classification of people's reaction to conflict. He puts people into five different types. There are those who react to conflict, problems, and change by hiding or refusing to deal with the problems. He calls these people **turtles**; they just hope the conflict will go away. There are those who react to conflict, problems, and change by giving in to the other person. He calls these people **teddy bears** in that they just want everyone to get along and they immediately will adapt to other's ideas, suggestions – even demands – if it will eliminate conflict. Another type of person is the person who reacts to conflict immediately, making it a competition that they need to win. He calls these people **sharks** in that they feel an internal need to oppose, attack, and stop those who don't totally agree with them. A fourth person that Shawchuck discusses is the person who is looking for options and ways for everybody to win. He calls these people **wise owls**. These people instinctively can see nuanced solutions and new paths that will allow everyone to gain. A fifth type of reaction to conflict, difficulty, and change are those who constantly seek to advance their position even if it is by a little bit. He calls these people **wily foxes**. These people are looking for some compromise in which their position advances. They do not care if others win, only that their position wins. They are willing to settle for less than all they want if they can get some of what they want. Different people have each of these natural reactions and only with skill can they be coaxed out of these situations into the appropriate one for the appropriate strategy. In many cases it is the **wise owls** who can help the most in working through difficult change but not in every case. Each of the above positions is an appropriate strategy depending on the change that is being proposed. The skillful leader will engage people within their natural style and seek to work with people to accomplish a righteous outcome. (Norman Shawchuck, *Managing Conflict Creatively*, 1990, William Carey Library)

It is crucial that you understand that everyone has a natural bent toward one of these styles of dealing with change, conflict, and problems. Leaders must know their people and draw people out past their natural reactions. Without these basic insights we might begin to dismiss people for their combativeness or lack of contribution when they may be able to make significant improvements to the idea being considered if they can be encouraged to move beyond their natural or learned style of interacting with change.

Basic Questions for Managing Change Through Communication

The following are a list of some of the questions that will help you think through the forms of communication that you could use that would allow the change to move forward as smooth as possible. For those of you who do not communicate naturally and constantly, these questions may be crucial to crystallizing your leadership. For those of you who do constantly communicate, these questions may become a launching pad to far more significant questions and actions.

Ô In what ways could we communicate about needed changes before actually starting to make changes?
Ô In what ways could we communicate as the changes are getting started?
Ô In what ways could we communicate about the changes that are in process as we are in the midst of the changes?
Ô In what ways could we communicate about changes that have been made?
Ô In what ways can we celebrate the changes that have been made?

Basic Questions for Managing Change Through Understanding Personalities

The following are a list of some of the questions that will help you think through the personalities of key people in your ministry organization that you could use to move forward as smooth as possible.

Ô Who in current leadership is an Early Adopter?
Ô Who in current leadership is a Middle Adopter?

Ô   Who in current leadership is a Late Adopter?
Ô   Who in current leadership is a Never Adopter?

Ô   Who in current leadership is a **turtle** when conflict arises?
Ô   Who in current leadership is a **teddy bear** when conflict?
Ô   Who in current leadership is a **wise owl** when conflict?
Ô   Who in current leadership is a **wily fox** when conflict?
Ô   Who in current leadership is a **shark** when conflict?

Advanced Techniques for Initiating and/or Managing Change

The following techniques can be adapted for initiating and managing change. These are additional ways of doing, asking, communicating, and understanding personalities. Look over each of these assistants to the change process and make them a part of your leadership skill set through experimentation and use.

Change Agents: Alignment Conversation

An alignment conversation is a conversation before an event, meeting, service, or week regarding each individual's expectations. "What are your expectations about this event, meeting, service, or week?" "I want to align our expectations in regard to this." "After this is over, what should have been accomplished?"

When the expectations are clear, then it is crucial to align everyone to those expectations. A clear alignment conversation can initiate needed change and help the smooth management of change. One executive asks his direct reports and every other employee in the company to write down the five most crucial actions they think they should be doing that week in order of importance and show that to their boss. This has allowed the whole company to be on the same page and striving for the same goals with the appropriate actions. He has them carry a card -- with the agreed upon five actions for the week -- with them at all times.

I am amazed at the power of this technique. Often it shows that two or more people are aiming at completely different objectives or they have completely different ideas about what needs to be done. If the expectations are clear and the actions are clear before an event or service or meeting, then success is almost assured. Another way to say this is, "If we were to be successful in _____, what will have happened?"

I can remember having this kind of conversation with a youth pastor on my staff in regards to the Thursday night junior high outreach gathering. I asked him what his expectations were for the evening. He said he wanted the twenty-five kids who came to feel welcome so they would invite their friends, to learn about the Bible and to grow spiritually. I said that I was expecting that seventy-five kids would come, many of which were non-Christians. This difference would never have been surfaced without my question. He and I were able to successfully interact about our different expectations and get on the same page.

Change Agents: Clarifying/Confronting Conversations

One of the ways to initiate positive change is to have an honest clarifying conversation about something that is not the way it should be. Pastors and church leaders are often very reticent to have these kinds of clear conversations. But it is essential that hard conversations take place at times. When something happens that is clearly wrong, inappropriate, or suspicious, someone needs to initiate a conversation that will get to the bottom of what really and truly happened. A clarifying conversation is what takes place after something bad, difficult, or troubling takes place. In a sense it is an alignment conversation after a bad event. Because something difficult, wrong, or problematic has taken place, the nature of the alignment is different. But it does need to be talked about.

The following eight-step process has proved helpful for many people in leadership positions:

1. Positive encouragement and praise
2. Statement that you could be wrong but…
3. Here is what I saw or heard
4. Tell me your side
5. We need to clear this up
6. What do you believe needs to be done?
7. Here are some other suggestions
8. We will do these things…

The **first** step is to make sure the other person knows that you notice and remember their positive points. This is usually best accomplished by stating some specific positive compliment or praise.

The **second** step of the clarifying process is to make the statement that you could be wrong or have misperceived. It is important that you acknowledge that it is possible that you do not have all your facts straight. There may be information, context, or something else that will change your opinion of what happened. Some people will not seek to clarify until they are sure that they are right; this often takes too long and means everyone has hardened into positions that they do not want to give up. There is a need for a candid conversation about what happened soon after it happened. It doesn't do any good to wait a month or more to have a conversation; that is why you must start with an admission that you could be wrong.

The **third** step is to say what you heard or saw or were told with as much detail as possible. Do not be subtle but state clearly what you saw, heard, or were told and why this is a problem. You have already said you could be wrong so you can state what you know with bluntness. The other person needs to know what you think they did or what is the problem. Do not allow the person to interrupt you and try and defend what you are saying until you are finished. Many times people will pick out a particular detail that may be inaccurate and try and get the whole discussion about that detail rather than the real issue. The person needs to know what you think and feel about the real issue.

The **fourth** step – after you have shared what you are concerned about and why you think it is wrong – is to let the other person tell you their side from beginning to end. Do not interrupt them except to ask questions. Let them tell their side of what happened and what led up to it. Take notes and pay attention to what they are saying and what they are not saying. This part of the process may take a while as they may be very upset that they have been caught or that they have been accused. If they have information that you did not have, then listen and look for ways to corroborate that information as you listen.

The **fifth** step – after thoroughly listening to their side – is to say, "We need to clear up what happened." It may be that you and they need to let people know that there has been a huge misunderstanding. It may be that you need to apologize to some people. It may be that they need to apologize to some people. There may be specific fixes and clean-ups that are specific to that situation. But this is a crucial step.

The **sixth** step is to ask the question, "What do you believe needs to be done to fix this?" It may be that step five is so determinative that step six is really a mute point. But the situation may be complex or involve multiple parties in such a way that you need to get all the parties input into how to clean up the difficulty.

The **seventh** step is to add other suggestions to what the other people come up with that will really make sure that a situation is handled and not swept under the rug. This step is where the leader would need to really give the details of an effective repentance plan in all its complexity if it has not been given earlier: How do we make sure that so and so are not still offended? How do we ensure that this event does not damage the reputation of Christ?

The **eighth** step is a step of commitment. This is where both sides agree to do what has been agreed upon so that the matter will be resolved, fixed, and forgiven. This is an important step in that it is a verbal or written commitment to do what has been agreed to in this meeting. Too often people have a meeting and then do not do anything that has been set up in the meeting.

Most people in our society do not know how to have the above kind of conversation, and so they wait until they are uncontrollably emotional and can no longer hold back with the offending individual. Leaders, however, must know how to have adult disagreements and corrective conversations with people. If a leader is mature and loving in the midst of this type of difficult conversation, people will appreciate them and follow them.

Change Agents: Use Your Authority or Power

There are times when it is appropriate for a leader to use the authority and power they have to make a change happen. This is true even if not everyone is fully on board with the change. Certain issues and decisions will never reach consensus and will require a decision maker to pick a direction. If a leader is not prepared to make a decision that is not universally approved, then no change that is controversial will ever be made. Leaders, at times, must lead with changes that are crucial for the health of a ministry. There will almost always be people who are not in favor of that change or the timing of the change. There are times when your position as a leader gives you the ability to decide.

Change Agents: Show Them the Need

Many people are motivated to join a cause or approve a change when they see the need. The problem must be clearly seen as a significant problem before solutions and change will be accepted. Many times leadership is guilty of living with a problem for a long period of time and then proposing a solution without having the whole congregation "feel" the problem. Some changes are not easy to embrace until the problem they are designed to fix is clearly understood.

One pastor dismissed his church early one Sunday morning to waiting buses so that they could take a tour of downtown and see the homeless, the prostitutes, and the destitute who needed their help. Many of these church folks had never ventured down to the mean streets of the town. When they saw the need they had all kinds of motivation to pitch in and help.

Change Agents: Show Them Potential Solutions to the Problem

Many people know of the problem and they feel bad about the issue, but they do not have a concrete way to get involved and make a difference. It is human nature to ignore a problem that has no solution. It is extremely motivating to see a solution that works. When people see that a solution to a problem is available and it is doable, then they often want to pitch in. When the problem seems too big or unsolvable, there is little motivation to change.

Change Agents: Rewards

All of us are willing to move in a new direction if the rewards are great enough. Those rewards may be monetary, emotional, mental, social, spiritual, relational, organizational, or any number of personal rewards. We too often overlook this very real motivation for change, and we only speak about altruistic motivations for change. Raises, time-off, prizes, retreats, books, trips, training, and tickets are all various forms of encouraging people to be for change.

It can be very helpful to look at all the benefits of a change and then talk openly and often about all of those benefits. Different people will embrace different rewards or benefits and support the proposed change. Almost every large building campaign uses this way of initiating change. All the various benefits of a new building to all the different age groups are mentioned. These are spoken about, written about, prayed about, and thought about numerous times. This gives people the ability to handle the changes that are needed to get to the rewards.

Change Agents: Inspire

In order to generate or maintain the change process, there is a need for inspiration and emotional energy. Inspiration often comes from seeing solutions being applied: children rescued, lives changed, marriages saved, and – most importantly – new life being embraced through surrender to Jesus Christ. We often are so focused on the future goal that we do not stop to celebrate what has already happened or what others before us have accomplished. There will always be future battles to be fought and future programs to be launched, but we must regularly remind ourselves of the good things that have happened because of what we are doing. We can then draw the connection to what that will look like in the future, in the new people. Inspire people by telling them what they and others have already achieved.

Change Agents: Consequences

One of the often overlooked or misused methods for motivating, and even managing, change is to show the consequences of what will happen if the present course is projected out over the next year or five years. If we do not want these consequences, then we must change course. The consequences must be made real and believable in order to create action in the present. One must cite examples, studies, Scriptural stories, logical extensions, etc. This leadership skill is really arguing your case in the minds of your hearers. Do you want these consequences? Do you like where the ministry is right now? How is your present system working for you?

If you are going to use consequences to create change, then this cannot be vague generalized difficulties. The more specific the bad results can be shown to be, the better it is in creating energy for change. Many organizations wait and use consequences as the final straw to try and bring about change in a person or department. If consequences are only used as punitive measures after the desired goals are not met, the full impact of this technique is not being utilized. It would be better to talk about these negative consequences early enough so that the person can change before they take effect. Help people see that the path they are on will end in disaster.

Change Agents: Clarity

There is something incredibly motivating about clarity. When the mission is crystal clear, it begs to be done. "Here is what we need to have happen." Many times the change that is desired is so fuzzy that we don't know what to do. We often say things like we want the church to grow. When we should say concrete things like, "We want one hundred people to become Christians in the next six months." "How do we make that happen?" "We want seventy-five junior high school students to attend a weekly gathering where they get exposed to the claims of Christ." "How do we make that happen?" "We want two hundred and fifty people reading their Bible and praying daily." "How do we make that happen?" Spend the extra time to make sure the goal is clear. Describe the goal to a number of people and ask them to repeat back to you what they think you want done. You are not clear enough until others can hear the goal and unerringly head toward the goal.

The military tries to make their mission goals clear enough that they can be carried out by the next level down if the leader is killed or captured. That is the level of clarity that is motivating. Make the goal or the mission abundantly clear so that it is easy to get on board. Colin Powell said "Leadership is about two things: the mission and the men." "What is the mission?" "Stopping the Russian Army from this tree to that tree." The only other question is "What do the men need to make that happen?" (General Colin Powell, February 24, 2009, Arco Arena, speech.)

Change Agents: Candor

This is where everyone is being very clear about what has happened, why it has happened, and what will happen if it does not change. This is also about each person's individual strengths and weaknesses. Too often we are in the business of spin or making things sound palatable or avoiding honest conversations about abilities and weakness. This leaves people confused about what is really happening.

It is difficult to let people know that they are being let go for poor performance or that a whole division is being closed because it is off mission or less important. It is difficult to not want to say something that sounds nice and is partially the truth rather than really giving people the whole truth.

It is never easy to be candid with someone about why they will not be promoted or given a particular assignment, but they often need this level of candor to make personal improvements or stay on the team. I remember having a conversation with a young lady who wanted to be considered for the leadership of a very successful children's program in our church. She was involved in leading one of the sub-ministries under this program. I asked her what she thought her spiritual gifts were and her God-given talents. She fairly accurately listed her strengths. Later in the conversation I asked her what she thought were the assignments involved in leading this particular children's ministry. We had a very detailed and thorough conversation about what was required to lead this program well. I had hoped that she would see that her gifts and talents did not line up with the leadership requirements of the ministry position. When she did not make that connection, I had to make that connection for her. I told her that I was committed to her being all that she could be as person and be for the Lord. I repeated her spiritual gifts and talents and excitedly projected those gifts and talents into a future of serving the Lord. Then I, matter of factly, showed her that her strengths did not line up with the ministry position that she was asking me to give her. I told her I could not give her the leadership position because it did not line up with her strengths. I told her that I wanted her to love ministry and serving the Lord and if I gave her this job, she would get burned out and probably resent me in six months to a year. I suggested many other opportunities in the church that perfectly matched her God-given gifts, talents, and abilities. She did not like the conversation because I was telling her no, but she stayed in the church and served the Lord much more effectively in a different position.

Change Agents: The Steps or a System

One of the very helpful ways to initiate change and manage it well is to write out or display the step-by-step system that will arrive at the desired goal. People can see the process and thereby be motivated to jump on board. People can see how they are deviating from the original plan and thereby may not allow the achievement of the goal. At times it is very helpful to have a number of people help in the creation of this step-by-step system or process so that they can contribute their wisdom. This brings a level of ownership and involvement to everyone involved. This writing down of a step-by-step process also allows people to see what may have been left out of a previous situation and/or where they may, at present, be about to make a mistake.

Let me be clear; almost everything any of us do is a part of a system. It may not be a very good system but underlying what we do is some form of: do this first; then do this; then do this; then do that. What is needed is to have effective pastors write down their mental system or list and then openly show the list to others who want to learn to do ministry. Writing down a proven, working system of effective ministry allows others to be recruited to join in. The system will be improved upon by others, but this is a part of what we are mandated to do. (2 Timothy 2:2)

Change Agents: Going to the Goal and Working Backward

Business, NASA, Stephen Covey, and hundreds of others have found that sometimes the best way to get something started and/or to maintain something well is to mentally go all the way to its completion and work backwards to the present period.

When the space program wanted to put a man on the moon and bring him back safely, they used this method. No one had ever attempted, let alone completed, a successful lunar landing and returned so a whole new series of processes, vehicles, and gadgets needed to be invented. They began by imagining an astronaut standing back on earth after having just completed a trip to the moon. They began asking questions like what had to happen right before he is standing on earth. They wrote down a number of answers and then they asked what had to happen before that could happen. Each answer told them another piece of what had to be invented, programmed, prepared, and scheduled to put a man on the moon and bring him back safely.

Many churches need to imagine the perfect worship service and work backwards and work out all the various steps, systems, and coordinated actions that must take place to make the perfect worship service happen. This can be used for special services throughout the year as well. It is often very motivational for people to see all that has to happen for a great service to happen.

This process can be used for existing systems and procedures also. If you will ignore what you are already doing and focus on your ideal outcome and work backwards, you will often see the flaws in your present system. This process can also give confidence that there will be perseverance toward a distant goal and not chasing new fads or quick fixes. Sometimes this process can show the few key steps that are missing that keep a project from getting launched or that cause it to consistently be derailed.

Change Agents: Participation or Part Ownership in the Vision

In the nonprofit world, the leader cannot give people bonuses or monetary incentives to buy into a project or goal. However, the idea of ownership and personal engagement is still powerful. If we give people the chance to put in their ideas and their refinements, their opposition often goes way down. The best political, educational, and charitable leaders do not personally produce a step-by-step road map to achieve a desired goal. They instead clearly define the goal or outcome and then invite people to go to work and show how to get there. If it will take everyone's cooperation to accomplish this goal then it requires everyone's input. Just the other day I heard a brilliant political leader point to a goal that all parties could agree on and then say, "Get to work and show us how to accomplish this." We all knew that he had specific ideas in mind, but he was wise enough not to share his specific ideas. He wanted buy-in from lots of people.

Change Agents: Expose the Fear and Break It

Many times we shrink back from the things that we know we need to change because of the fears that arise in our heads. All of us have fears, assumptions, and beliefs that keep us from attempting things. Every time we hear or think of something wonderful, in a very short period of time all kinds of fears and reasons it won't work pop into our minds. It is those fears and reasons that will stop us from pursuing this new direction. It can be very helpful to ask people to write down their fears and reasons why this won't work and then examine those issues. If you can attack the fear and the reasons with solid answers, then it is much easier to move forward with the needed change.

This is how a huge elephant is controlled by a small stake and a little rope. When the elephant was small, it was tied with a small rope to a small stake in the ground. Because the baby elephant could not pull the stake loose, the adult elephant assumes that the same size stake is unmovable. In the same way we have "learned," in the past, that certain things shouldn't be tried and so we pass over options, ideas, and solutions that would work. In some cases it is important to bring these fears, assumptions, and beliefs out into the open and talk about them. Demonstrate that they are not true. Give examples that debunk their controlling power. Too often we allow these fears, assumptions, and beliefs to remain hidden and unspoken which is the key to their power over our thinking.

Change Agents: Talk About the Elephant in the Room

In some cases an organization, department, church, or small group is held hostage to truth that no one wants to talk about. It may be the incompetence of the leader; it may be an unethical practice; it may be favoritism, racism, class-ism; it may be the failure or idiocy of a program or product; or any number of other elephants in the room. When an organization, ministry, or department cannot talk about what is obviously a problem, then movement toward a goal is sabotaged, blocked, or slowed.

It is often helpful to have an elephant-in-the-room exercise. This is where everyone is handed small slips of paper and they are asked to write down what they think is the elephant in the room. This is an anonymous process where everyone can be completely candid about the problem no one is willing to talk about.

There was a time in my ministry when my incompetence administratively was the elephant in the room. Finally the board of my church just started talking about it and the need to make a change. They eventually asked me to elevate the youth pastor to executive pastor so that things would stop falling through the cracks and there would be the proper amount of management and administration.

Change Agents: Care

Care deeply for the people who report directly to you, and it will increase their willingness to carry out your expectations. All organizations can become so task oriented that the people become just tools to accomplish the organizational tasks. When people feel like they are just pieces of equipment to their leaders, there will be much less achieved. This "technique" requires that a leader spend time learning and listening to their direct reports. What are their hobbies? What are their aspirations outside of work? What are the names and interests of their family? What are they struggling with? What is going right in their life? Sometimes these are water cooler conversations. Sometimes they are a natural part of the business meeting. But the people who actually make a church work must sense in their bones that they are cared about.

People need to know that their leader cares for them and their leader knows and wants what is best for them. Do they have tangible evidence that they are more than a human piece of equipment? The largest study ever done on effective management by the Gallop organization says that one of the top four things that must be true of the leaders of departments, divisions, and companies is "You must show care for your people." (Marcus Buckingham, *The One Thing You Need to Know*, Free Press, A Division of Simon and Schuster, Inc. 1230 Avenue of the Americas, New York, NY., p 79)

Change Agents: Mission Drift

It is easy to drift away from the mission of the organization if you are not regularly checking back in with the mission/purpose/values. This must happen at least every six months. This discussion must engage the people in the organization with how they will help accomplish the mission of the organization in the next period. If they do not engage with the mission, then they will not see how their part is a part of the larger whole.

In the church the mission or purpose of the church is clear. It is Evangelism – bringing lost people to the Savior; Discipleship – helping people learn Jesus' way of living and loving in every arena of life; Worship – exalting God through word and deed; Fellowship – Drawing closer to the Lord and others for encouragement and support; Compassion – tangible evidence of the love of Christ to the poor, afflicted, and oppressed. Since this is our mission, it is important to have the leaders and team members of each ministry answer the question, "How are you all planning on doing these purposes in the next six months?" Everyone on the team must understand that what they do contributes to these ultimate purposes.

Evangelism	Discipleship	Worship	Fellowship	Compassion

Change Agents: Evaluation

Churches and nonprofit organizations regularly overlook the value of evaluation. They are always short on staff and resources, so they are forced to move on to the next assignment because the needs just keep coming. Evaluation is key to improvement. In other words, looking at the Sunday service and really saying what went right; what went wrong; what could be improved. It means looking at a video of the children's ministry and showing what went right, what went wrong, and what could be improved. It means really observing the ushers and greeters and seeing what they actually do and say. It means sending out cards to newcomers so that they can evaluate the service that they just attended. The following are some of the evaluation questions that can be asked to determine what needs to be improved, discarded, redirected, or left alone.

Evaluate the Vision
- Ô   What is your vision?
- Ô   Is your vision compelling?
- Ô   Is your vision appropriate for your organization?

Evaluate the Systems
- Ô What is your system for …?
- Ô (assimilation, discipleship, evangelism, etc.)
- Ô Is your system effective for producing the result?
- Ô What needs to be changed, added, or deleted?
- Ô Do you need a whole new system?

Evaluate the Personnel
- Ô Who is in place to lead the process?
- Ô Can they accomplish the goals?
- Ô Are they accomplishing the goals?
- Ô Should this person be moved, motivated, or released?

Evaluate the Impact
- Ô Is the purpose being accomplished by the process?
- Ô Is the vision becoming true?
- Ô Was our system effective at meeting the need and/or accomplishing the vision?
- Ô Did we accomplish anything with all the activity?
- Ô Did we accomplish the expectations that we set?
- Ô Were they the right expectations?

Change Agents: There is No Such Thing as Problem Free

There is the myth in church and charitable organizations that there are solutions, programs, and methodologies that are problem free. But this is not true. Every potential solution will have problems associated with it. Leadership involves picking your problems. Which problems are you willing to live with? Some critics believe that all they have to point out are the problems and this renders a new goal as undesirable. This is not true, however, because every direction has problems. The present problem is that we have grown comfortable with our current problems and the new direction involves problems that we are uncomfortable with.

I know of two churches where they were playing loud worship music which was very offensive to a certain group of people. In one of the churches a man confronted the pastor about the loudness of the music. The pastor very tactfully but assertively thanked the man for his comments but said, "This is the kind of music that we use for worship." "There are lots of other churches in town that play the kind of music you would like to hear." "We are trying to reach people who enjoy worshipping to this kind of music." The pastor of the other church had a completely different response when the loudness of the music was railed against. He told the sound people and the musicians to tone down the music so as not to offend people who don't like loud worship music. Both pastors had problems even after this, but one had the problem of lots of loud, young people coming to worship. The other had the problem of an aging congregation with definite ideas about everything.

Conclusion

The leadership group of every church must be able to initiate needed change and must be able to manage the change process. These are skills, not gifts. They can be learned. Yes, some people will be more naturally talented at these skills than others. But the person who is practiced at these skills is better than the talented but unpracticed. It is important to realize that you can grow in the use of these skills.

On the next few pages you will find a quick summary of the ways of initiating and managing change that were discussed in this chapter. Some leaders have found it helpful to put these reminders under the glass on their desk and then be able to refer to them when they need to at critical change moments. NO leader is naturally skilled at all of these, and we need to keep growing and keep practicing.

Initiating Change

Doing

Asking

Managing Change

Communication

Communication before the change

Communication during the change

Communication after the change

Personalities

Reactions to new

Early adopter

Middle adopter

Late adopter

Never adopter

Natural reactions to conflict and opposition

Turtle

Teddy bear

Wise owl

Wily fox

Shark

Advanced Techniques

1. Alignment conversations

2. Clarifying/confronting conversations

1. Positive encouragement and praise.

2. Statement that you could be wrong, but…

3. Here is what I saw or heard.

4. Tell me your side.
5. We need to clear this up.
6. What do you believe needs to be done?
7. Here are some other suggestions.
8. We will do these things…

3. Use authority or power

4. Show them the need

5. Show them potential solutions to the problem

6. Rewards

7. Inspire

8. Consequences

9. Clarity

10. Candor

11. The steps or a system

12. Going to the goal and working backward

13. Participation or part ownership in the vision

14. Expose the fear and break it

15. Talk about the elephant in the room

16. Care

17. Mission drift

18. Evaluation

19. There is no such thing as problem free

LEADERSHIP SKILL #6 – DEVELOP PEOPLE SKILLS
Seven People Skills Needed for Leadership

Think back on your experience of junior high school. What comes to mind? Many people's memories of junior high school involve being picked on, embarrassed, fear, doubt, low self-esteem, bullying, etc. Junior high was a brutal period for many. Like sharks smelling blood, the other students attack any weakness; real or imagined. If you had a flaw, it was noticed and used against you. The name of the game in junior high was step on others to make yourself look good. Junior high was also a time of intense self-focus. Everything was evaluated by whether it benefited you personally. The tragedy is that over eighty percent of us never recover from the people skills we learned in junior high. If we are going to become good leaders, then we must unlearn the lessons of junior high. A junior high orientation towards others cripples your leadership. Great leaders shed those negative "skills."

Leave behind childish notions about how to get ahead and about forcing people to do what you want. It is childish to believe that leadership is earned by putting people down or focusing on limitations. Real leadership begins to emerge when other people are seen for their strengths, their value, and their innate dignity. People become ardent followers of those people who see them for their value, their strengths, and always try and put them in the best possible position.

Leadership means working with people. If you have great ideas but can't work with people, you are not a leader. One of the most significant jumps in your leadership ability takes place when you become skilled at interacting positively with people. Just as there are techniques for working with metal, wood, and chemicals, so there are ways of working with people. Most of us were not trained in these "ways of dealing with people" when we were growing up. This chapter outlines seven basic people skills that every leader should be able to execute naturally and with ease.

Remember Jesus said that Christian leaders were not going to lord it over their followers (Matthew 20:25-27). Christian leaders are supposed to use their position to serve and develop their followers while at the same time still accomplishing the larger kingdom goal. Christian leaders are supposed to love their followers. Christian leaders are not supposed to be focused on their own fame, power, or money but the well-being of their followers. Christian leaders take the time to teach people how to live a life full of love. This form of leadership – often called servant leadership – is desperately needed in our day. Christian leaders should be known for their willingness to serve those they have been asked to lead. Servant leadership is a form of love and this is now called people skills. People skills are not manipulation techniques although they can be used that way. People skills are ways to love others in a work environment. People skills are ways to want the best for the individuals while at the same time accomplishing great things organizationally. When a follower is under a person with people skills they are energized, developed, stretched, and loved. They often say that the years under that leader were some of the best in their life.

In any organization all real work takes place with and through people. People are not robots that can be programmed to complete a task and then ignored except for regular maintenance.

Unfortunately this is how many organizations – even churches – treat people. Skilled leaders are able to work with people, motivate people, and influence people. People are not tools for accomplishing the leader's goals. People are the goal and the means to the goal. No organization can describe itself as a winner if it reaches the finish line and everyone on the team hates each other.

The Seven Essential People Skills

There are literally hundreds of unique and valuable people skills, but the seven that we will discuss in this chapter are bedrock foundations of any leadership success with people. The seven people skills that we will cover are:

First, add value to others constantly. Focus on the value of others. People with the "gift" of charisma are those who enter a room focused on other people, not themselves.

Second, stop complaining, criticizing and condemning. No one picks friends who put them down even if they deserve it; we get away from those people.

Third, T.A.P. people as often as you can. (Thankful; Appreciative; Praise). We all are drawn to people who appreciate us, thank us regularly, and are truly grateful for any and everything we do.

Fourth, add value to the other person every time you are with them. Honor and respect are not easy to come by in our world; but if you are giving it away constantly, people line up to receive it from you.

Fifth, focus on people's strengths instead of their weaknesses. Most people in their own mind allow their good points to dominate their thinking. If we are going to connect with them, then that is where we must start every time.

Sixth, ask questions about the other person wants and/or interests. People are drawn to others who help them accomplish their goals, so find a way that their goals and your goals line up.

Seventh, apologize when you are wrong. When we freely admit mistakes and faults, people love us more not less. These skills are not exotic or revolutionary. But they are so essential that ignoring them will immediately diminish your leadership potential.

People Skill #1 – Add value to others

One of the best examples of effective people skills is a woman I have known for over thirty years. We will call her Diana. She was not especially attractive, but everyone was attracted to her. Diana constantly made people feel valuable and important. In college she had an endless string of attractive men clamoring for her attention. She picked a very handsome man and let him marry her. In the work place she was always consulted because you left a meeting with her, feeling more intelligent. When you were with her your importance, your ideas, your goals, and your successes became the focus. She was reticent to correct you; but on the few occasions that she did, it was clear that it was your success that was most prominent in her mind. She always seemed fascinated to listen to your ideas or concerns. She asked penetrating questions which let you know she was listening intently. When you did something positive or in the direction she thought was best, she would never let you forget it. On the few occasions that she made mistakes, her abject horror and contrition forced you to forgive her as quickly as you could. I do not know whether Diana came by her people skills naturally or learned them, but people deferred to her leadership because of them.

Being skilled with people is all about acknowledging their value and adding to that value. Like the house plant unerringly turns toward the sun, so people always turn toward the person, boss, friend, and leader who will shine value on and into their life. We want to be with people who make us feel special. We need to be with people who increase our value. If you decide to start giving value, meaning, and significance away, people will be much more open to your leadership. One could say that all of the techniques we are detailing in this chapter are ways to add value. In every relationship in our life people are looking for value – respect – honor – a feeling of importance. This feeds our soul.

Why do some teenagers turn towards their friends for advice rather than their parents? Because their friends give them more value and respect than their parents, in most cases. Why do some pastors work seventy-plus hours every week and neglect their families? Because they receive more respect and value from the people at church than the members of their family. Why do some men play golf for six hours every Saturday rather than spend time with their family? Because they are receiving more honor and respect from playing golf with the guys than they would at home. Why do some women and men get involved romantically with someone outside of their marriage? Because there is more respect, value, and honor coming from the illicit relationship than from their marriage. If we want to lead well and with joy, then we must learn how to add value to the people in our life. Add value to people every time you are with them. Keep your mind and heart alert for ways to add value to people in your life. Practice on everyone.

The Bible says, "Honor all men, love the brotherhood, fear the king" (1 Peter 2:17). It tells husbands to honor their wives (1 Peter 3:7) and wives to respect their husbands (Ephesians 5:33). It instructs us to, "give preference to one another in honor." (Romans 12:10). It tells children to "Honor their father and their mother" so that their life will be blessed. (Exodus 20:12) The word honor means to add value. God commands us to speak, act, and design ways for people to have more value when they are with us. This makes us people magnets. People crave this added value. God commands that we give it to others and it costs us nothing to add value to others, so why don't we do this constantly? We often want our importance to be noticed by the other person before we acknowledge theirs. Jesus however said, "Do unto others what you would have them do unto you." (Matthew 7:12)   He, in essence, tells us to go first.

Let me give you the other side of that story. Have you ever been around a person who sucks value out of your life: a boss, colleague, classmate, or parent who always points out what you did wrong; a person who revels in pointing out your weaknesses; someone who puts you down, ignores you, or is dismissive of you. Avoid these people if possible. They steal joy.

Leadership for a Change Exercise

Ô   Add value to five people in your life today.
Ô   Write a postcard or email thanking them for something they did; compliment them with specific compliments.
Ô   Purchase a little gift, card, or memento which says I appreciate you.
Ô   Tell someone else that these people are important to you.

People Skill #2 – Focus on others; forget yourself

Imagine that you are just entering a room full of people all standing around with the program about to start in fifteen minutes. The room has people you know well, people you know casually, and people you don't know at all. What kinds of internal thoughts fill your mind?

"What are they thinking about me?"
"How do I look?"
"Who's noticing me?"
"Don't do anything embarrassing!"
"Who would I like to talk to?"

If you allow this kind of self talk to dominate your thinking then you damage, if not destroy, your ability to lead. This orientation creates no energy and thus no charisma.

If, on the other hand, you force yourself to think these questions:

"What do these people need to have a good time?"
"What would cause these people to relax or laugh?"
"What does this person want to talk about?"
"What would be interesting to this person?"
"How can I make sure that these people are comfortable?"

Then you have opened a secret way of thinking that few have mastered. Everyone, whether they are naturally outgoing or introverted, must learn this key secret of charisma.

John Maxwell, in his lectures, consistently states that the key to charisma is to walk into a room thinking about **_OTHERS_** not yourself. If you force your focus to be on others, people will naturally be attracted to you. An intense focus on others is the best working definition for charisma. This switch in your approach is an absolutely key change that will allow you to be a leader.

Jesus says that the two great commandments are to love God and to love others. To fulfill these commands means that our focus is on God and others and not on ourselves. Jesus is essentially saying that if we focus on meeting the needs, pursuing, and pleasing God and others, then we will have a fulfilling and satisfying life.

Focusing on others is a skill that can be developed. It does not come naturally or easily. Do not cop out and say that you are not naturally interested in others. No one is. In fact, the Bible tells us that everyone is naturally self-focused, selfish, and sinful (Romans 3:23). Overcoming this natural selfishness and self-focus requires surrender to Jesus Christ as the Savior and Lord of your life.

Scripture says, *Do nothing from selfish ambition or empty conceit but with humility of mind let each of you regard one another as more important than himself. Do not merely look out for your own personal interests but also for the interest of others.* Philippians 2:1-4. *All things are lawful, but not all things are profitable. All things are lawful, but not all things edify.* <u>*Let no one seek his own good, but that of his neighbor.*</u> 1 Corinthians 10:23,24

When you are talking with someone, drop all hope of steering a conversation to what interests you and drill into what interests them. Follow their line of thinking wherever it goes. Sometimes you can write down a thought or topic for later. But many times it is better to just let your thoughts and topics recede and follow their line of thinking.

Have you ever spent time with someone who is trying to impress you with how much they know? Are you impressed? NO!!! They are saying, "Notice me or I will derail every conversation with my comments and knowledge until someone notices me." On the other hand, have you spent time with someone who draws you out with their questions on your subject? Don't you want to spend more time with that person? Instead of trying to impress people with how impressive you are, impress people with how interested you are in them.

It takes a high level of discipline to set aside all the things you would like to talk about; all the reactions that come to your mind; and instead focus on the other person's life, topic, and interests. Great leaders are others focused and ask question after question to the people in front of them. These questions shout, "I care about you and what you do." It is amazing what you can learn and the warmth that you communicate.

Let me say a word of balance. It can sound like I am saying that we need to give whoever we happen to be with unlimited time, focus, and care. No!!! We all have ten major relationships in our life: God, Self, Marriage, Family, Work, Church, Friends, Finances, Society, Enemies. Each of the people in these relationships does not get equal amounts of time, resources, or information. We have to give time, resources, and information out in a priority order. When you focus on others, make sure that you direct this intense focus to the most important people in your life.

Leadership for a Change Exercise

Every time you are with someone today, put in the mental, emotional, and physical energy to focus on them.

Ask them questions until they don't want to talk about the subject anymore.

- Ô   Stop and listen to the answers people are trying to tell you.
- Ô   Notice things about them.
- Ô   Do not tell your stories or what their comments remind you of.
- Ô   Stay on the topic that interests them without changing it to your topic.
- Ô   If they ask about you, gently demure and ask another question about them.

People Skill #3 – Stop complaining, criticizing, or condemning

I was shocked one day, watching the news, when a man who had imprisoned and violated his own daughter for twenty-four years in a small room in the basement prepared to plead not guilty to the charges laid against him. He repeatedly stated that he was not a monster even though he had killed one of his daughter's children and threatened all of them with death if they tried to escape. He was, by everyone's account, a monster with no conscience. But he saw himself as a good person with a little problem. His rationalized his actions, inflated his good points, and was not open to criticism or condemnation. If this kind of man is reluctant to criticize himself or let others condemn him, then we can understand why criticism, condemnation, and complaining do not work with regular people who make normal mistakes and errors.

Most people instinctively know to get away from a person who constantly points out the flaws, problems, and mistakes of others. We know that this person is saying negative things about us when we are not around. Realize that people will not be drawn to you if you are a critic. It does not matter if you are right.

There is a time for criticism and clear-eyed assessment of reality. But people follow leaders who know when to withhold criticism and when to give it. We usually do not want to follow someone who is all criticism. If you constantly are critical, you will diminish your leadership ability.

People need a lot of positive comments and a lot of attention on what they did right. There is an interesting statistic that the average person receives thirty-two negative comments for every one positive comment in their life. It is remarkable what happens when you turn this around for people. Just stopping the negative flow out of your mouth causes people to like you and then if you add a sincere and real appreciation, people are drawn to you.

The Bible says in Philippians 2:14, *Do all things without grumbling or disputing.* Colossians 3:8 states, *But now you also, put them all aside: anger, wrath, malice, slander, and abusive speech from your mouth.* Look at how the Apostle Paul talks about the impact of negative speech in Galatians 5:15, *But if you bite and devour one another, take care that you are not consumed by one another.* Jesus says, *Judge not lest you be judged.* (Matthew 7:1) We all know of Jesus' comments that we should not try and pick the speck out of our brother's eye until we have removed the log from our own. All of these Scriptures are trying to tell us to tone down or eliminate the negative comments.

Leadership that works eliminates negative comments as much as possible. Everyone can see the problems; leaders see the positives and the solutions. Cut people more slack. People need to know what they did right and what they have going for them.

Leadership for a Change Exercise

Ô For the next week you are not allowed to criticize, complain, or condemn anyone for anything. You must let it go.

Ô Reverse the thirty-two negative comments to one good comment with your family and colleagues this week.

People Skill #4 – T. A. P. People -- thankful, appreciative, praise people

Everyone loves being thanked, appreciated, and praised (T.A.P.). One of the secrets of my church's making a turnaround from all the splits and negativity of its past was creating an incredibly positive atmosphere through postcards. I went to a seminar where the speaker gave the assignment for each of us to spend the first thirty minutes of each work week writing as many positive postcards as we could. I was able to write about thirty to forty of them in thirty minutes. I let the folks in the office address them. This meant that each week I would mail out thirty to forty encouraging, positive, and complimentary postcards to people in the church.

If I had seen any positive action the previous week, I would write a little note of thanks and appreciation. I was shocked at the difference it began to make. When I would go to people's homes they would have my postcard on the refrigerator. One person told me that the reason they could keep serving, in spite of all the dumb stuff at the church, was my postcards. When we added staff, they were required to spend the first thirty minutes of their work week writing positive postcards. This became so popular that we asked the lay leaders to write thirty or more postcards every week. With each successive new group of folks who started writing positive postcards in our church, a whole new positive vibe swept over the church. We started to catch people doing things right all the time. It was a great place to come to church because people were regularly praising you for things they saw you do. You were being noticed and appreciated.

One of the simplest but most profound people skills is to T.A.P. people at every opportunity: This means to be thankful, appreciative, and full of sincere praise. Look for opportunities to be T.A.P. people Play a game and T.A.P. as many people as possible each day with a comment, a note, a letter or a phone call. Watch what happens. You will be astounded.

A number of years ago I was training a pastoral intern in the absolute necessity of being thankful, appreciative, and full of praise. He began writing postcards and being more openly positive. He asked if there was a danger of doing this too much. I answered that, "It could only be too much if it was insincere or was not tied to an actual positive contribution a person had made." I told him to only write about the positive he heard or saw and it would never be too much.

People are genuinely starved for praise and appreciation. If your organization is known for praising people instead of criticizing them, people will be drawn to you. I mentioned this as I was consulting with a church that had a very negative history. The church was known for devouring staff and lay leaders through critical comments. They agreed to try my positive postcards idea. It completely changed their church.

Look at what the Scripture says in Ephesians 4:29, *Let no unwholesome word proceed from your mouth, but only such a word as is good for edification according to the need of the moment, so that it will give grace to those who hear.* We all are drawn to people who appreciate us, thank us regularly, and are truly grateful for any and everything we do.

In an interesting book called *The Truth About Cheating,* M. Gary Newman suggests that over ninety percent of men who cheat on their wives do so because they felt "emotionally disconnected and <u>underapprecia</u>ted by their wives." Take this as a general truism; we move toward those who appreciate and praise us, and we move away from those who undervalue us and/or disrespect us. We do this even if we know it is wrong to move towards the person who is praising us.

One wise leader said, "I have yet to find the person, however great or exalted his station, who did not do better work and put forth greater effort under a spirit of approval than he would ever do under a spirit of criticism." (Dale Carnegie, *How to Win Friends and Influence People,* Pg 25)

This is a very simple lesson, but it works at all levels and with all kinds of people. T.A.P people with thanks, appreciation, and praise and you will begin to rise above the pack as a leader. Everyone has actions, words, attitudes, and intentions that are worthy of praise. They are hoping that someone will notice. Whoever notices has their attention and usually their loyalty.

Leadership for a Change Exercise

Ô Write thirty postcards or emails on Monday morning, first thing. One or two sentences of thanks, appreciation, or praise and mail them out. Do this every week and watch what happens.

Ô Reverse the nine-to-one rule: Most people hear nine negative comments to every one positive comment. You cannot make a critical comment until you have in some way communicated nine positive comments about this person.

People Skill #5 – Focus on people's strengths instead of their weaknesses and limitations

Quiz

List five people at work – what three things do you think about most when you think of them?

	Name or Initials	Three traits or characteristics
1.		
2.		
3.		
4.		
5.		

Did you find yourself mentally categorizing people for their strengths and good points or for their flaws and weaknesses?

Everyone needs to feel that they are important, noticed, and applauded. Good leaders get people focusing on each person's strengths rather than weaknesses. The effective leader has a laser-like focus on people's strengths and bringing those to bear in an organization. Those who speak well should be speaking. Those who organize well should be organizing. Those who plan well should be planning. Those who write well should be writing. This sounds so obvious that it doesn't need to be said. But it needs to be said over and over again. He/she also does what is possible to hide a person's weakness or make them irrelevant.

Focus on Strengths in Scripture

God has recognized this strengths orientation. He makes each person strong and weak in different ways: mentally, emotionally, physically, and spiritually (Psalm 139:13-16). He gives specific spiritual abilities to specific people so that they would use them to advance His kingdom purposes (Romans 12:3-8). It is tragic if leaders do not make sure that the spiritual strength of each individual Christian is harnessed for kingdom advancement.

If you are the leader who has the best interest of the organization and the individual in mind, then you will move people into positions and situations where their best will be on display. This requires hard conversations at times to move people into new roles, new positions, and new situations where their gifts are going to shine. But people and organizations thrive when you, as the leader, put people in the position to do what they do best.

When your focus is on people's strengths and maximizing those for the organization's and the individual's benefit, everybody wins. Yes, you will at times have to hide significant weaknesses in a person but that is what teams, assistants, and partners are for.

Leadership for a Change Exercise

Ô   What are five personality strengths of each of your team members?

Ô   What are five talent strengths of each of your team members?

Ô   What are five emotional strengths of your team members?

Ô   What are five spiritual strengths or gifts of your team members?

Ô   Tell them what you notice about them.

Ô   What are five workplace situations where your people could succeed?

Ô   Put them in a position this week to succeed.

People Skill #6 – Find out what the other person wants; what interests them; what they desire

In order to be a great leader, you must learn the secret of the fishermen. Fish are attracted to what interests them, not what interests the fisherman. Too often leaders throw out what they're interested in and expect people to be excited about it because they are the leader. This is naïve at best.

If I want to lead people to do a great work for God, then they must see what I am going to do as a way to accomplish what they want. What do they want? What are their interests? What do they desire? What are their goals? How does what I am trying to accomplish help individuals who follow me? If you can't answer these questions, then you won't be able to attract them to help you accomplish your plans and goals.

This idea of leading through helping others is a core idea in what Jesus was saying about the two great commandments (Mark 12:29-31) and His statements about servant leadership (Luke 22:26). Jesus stated that the two great commandments – which sum up all that God wants us to do in life – is to love God and love others.

If we are going to be leaders, we must escape the gravity of our own wants and interests and be about other people. I am amazed at how often we all violate this principle. We want people to like us, follow us, or engage with us and yet we lead with what interests us or what we want. It is counterintuitive to realize that we can get everything we righteously want if we will focus on what others want, but it is true.

The curse of our sin nature is that we are all self-focused and naturally most interested in what we want and what we need. This natural bias towards ourselves is a huge barrier to effective people skills. But if this knowledge of others can be harnessed, it can become one of the most powerful aids to leadership and team building. People do what they believe will yield what they want. Many times they are wrong, but that is why they do what they do, live the way they live, say what they say, and so on. Therefore it is the leaders job to help people see how following the leader's plan will allow people to gain what they really want. If they can accomplish everything they want to accomplish in life by joining you, then they will get on board.

I know of pastors and business leaders who want to lead their people forward; but all they can talk about is what they want, the programs, and ideas that excite them. This is a clear recipe for disaster. In order to succeed you must think about what the other person wants. This is the only reason why another person will do something. They want to.

Find a topic that the other person wants to talk about and stay on that topic until the other person changes the subject. Talk about, ask questions about, and show interest in what the other person wants and/or is interested in. It is only after you have listened to the other person's topic that they may be willing to listen to you on your topic. It is a sacrifice to sublimate your interests and desires and focus on the other person. But this sends all the right signals so that the person will want a relationship with you and will listen to you when the time is right.

Help people accomplish their goals, dreams, and desires

The second half of the great commandments is to love your neighbor as yourself. Life works when we help others accomplish their righteous desires, dreams, and goals. Stop trying to accomplish your goals first and then help others with the overflow. Understand what the other person wants and formulate your goals in terms of how they will help the person accomplish their goals. If it is clear that you want them to win, then they will want you to win. Find a way to weld together the different wants of the individual's and the organization's goals. Then a whole new level of energy will be released.

How do your goals for the organization help the individuals that work for you accomplish their dreams, their interests, and their desires? Do they get extra time off if they accomplish these? Do they get a bonus if the goals are accomplished? Do they get recognition, rewards, or gifts if they do a good job?

Leadership for a Change Exercise

- Ô   What do the people in your life righteously want?
- Ô   Spouse, children, boss, colleagues, subordinates, friends, etc.
- Ô   Learn those things and engage them on those issues.
- Ô

People Skill #7 – Apologize often and when you are wrong

A number of years ago I destroyed the engine in my car because I forgot to add oil. The car ran for a while on low oil until at one point it had no oil at all, and all the moving parts started heating up quickly and then gouged, melted, broke, and bashed into one another. Without oil everything about my car stopped working. The engine of a car is a fury of moving parts, explosions, and friction. So are most relationships. Apologies are the oil between hard edges of people. Without regular apologies our relationships can seize up. The apology has become a forgotten skill for getting along with people. People make mistakes. People are rude and offensive. People can intentionally and unintentionally get in the way. Everything that is true of others is also true for you. You can make mistakes. You can be rude and offensive. You can intentionally and unintentionally get in the way. Therefore you must always be ready to apologize. Some apologies are complicated, but most apologies are quick interactions that allow people to continue to work together. "I am sorry, please forgive me; I will try and do better." Say this often and especially when you have offended someone.

Look at what the Scripture says about this area

Jesus hits this theme of apology and relational friction a number of times. In Matthew 5:24, He says that if you have done something to offend another person then making it right takes priority even over worshipping God. This is serious stuff.

On another occasion, Matthew 18:15, Jesus states that if someone offends you seriously, then you must educate them about what they did so that they can apologize and this incident can be put behind you.

On a third occasion, Luke 17:3, Jesus tells His disciples to be on their guard that when someone offends you or you offend someone else, these slights and wounds must not be shoved under the rug as though they were no big deal. There must be education, apology, and reconciliation between people or the relationship will break down. Relational breakdown happens over time one small offense at a time until eventually you come to dislike the person.

What are the essential components of a more thorough apology?

There are two kinds of an apology. The short uncomplicated, "I'm sorry, please forgive me; I will try and do better" apology. This type of apology fixes inadvertent, small offenses. The other type of apology is complicated and deep because the offense was serious, repetitive, and scaring. The more thorough apology unfolds usually in a typical six-step format:

The **first** part of a more thorough apology is a gentle non-defensive manner. This means that your tone of voice, your attitude, your manner is humble, contrite, and gentle (Proverbs 15:3). Maintain a gentle non-defensive manner.

The **second** aspect of a deeper apology is seeking education. This means that you ask the other person to help you understand how you have hurt them. Admit that you have clearly offended them and do not want to do it again. Admit that you probably do not understand all the ways that you have offended them. Ask them to educate you so you won't do it anymore. They need to tell you what you did, and they need to see you receive it. This may take forty-five minutes or longer.

The **third** aspect of a thorough apology is a willingness to admit you were wrong. You must own up to what you did or did not do, even if it was in response to what the other person did. "I was wrong when I did such and such or said this or that." "I should not have gotten angry like I did and pounded the table." It is always helpful to be specific.

The **fourth** aspect of a thorough apology is to ask for their forgiveness. "Would you forgive me?" Sometime it is more appropriate to say, "I know that I do not have any right to ask that you would forgive me but would you forgive me?" This can only come after you have admitted that what you did was wrong.

The **fifth** aspect of a deeper apology is to enact a repentance plan. If your offense was very serious or has been repeated a number of times, enlist the other person in helping you change. I call this a repentance plan. You might say something like, "I do not want to do that anymore, so would you be willing to hold me accountable on this issue?"

The **sixth** aspect of an effective deep apology is to test for openness. If an apology worked, then the person will be open to discussing other matters and sharing a lighter or even more personal side of themselves with you. If they are willing to talk with you about it, that means that the apology worked and the normal working relationship has been restored.

Leadership for a Change Exercise

- Ô Write down the names of three to five people to whom you probably should apologize.
- Ô Apologize to them.
- Ô Put all seven people skills on a little card that you put in your pocket. Take the card out and review it before and after every meeting you have for a week. Watch what happens when you continue this habit of reminding yourself of basic people skills before every get-together.

LEADERSHIP SKILL #7 - WISDOM: WISE DECISIONS

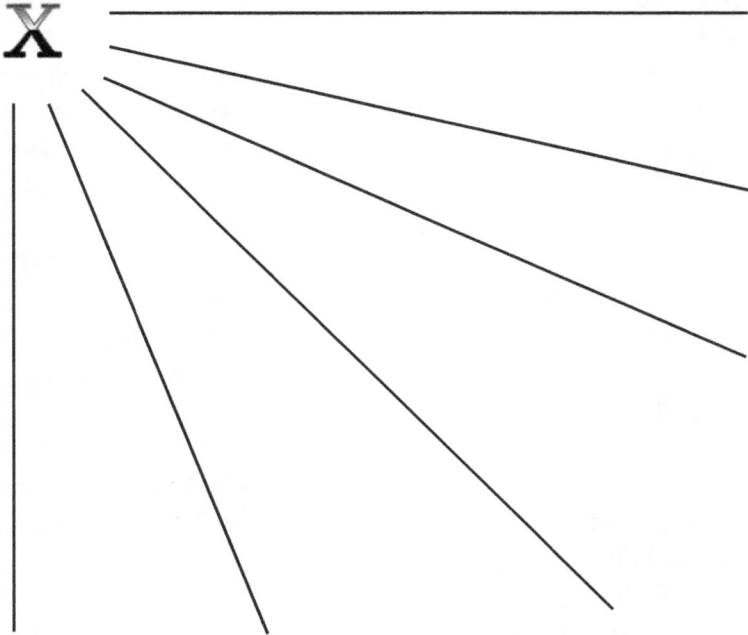

    You are facing a major decision: a new hire, an acquisition, a job change, an employee termination, a new strategy, a financial downturn. X marks the spot where you are now. The lines are the various results of the decision you could make. The question you need answered is, "What is the best decision?" Do you take the opportunity or not. How do you know what to do? How can you be sure of the wisest course of action? There are three things you know for sure. You must choose one of them. Whichever one you choose eliminates the other possibilities. Your life will be different whichever one you choose.

Leaders must be ready to make decisions all the time. They must become good at picking out the right course of action. Leaders must succeed in their decisions more than most or someone else will be asked to make the decisions. This chapter looks at how to make the best decision. This is called WISDOM. In our modern era it is called decision making. I think we have much to learn about developing this skill from the ancient biblical perspective.

Go back with me three-thousand years as King Solomon tells us that wisdom is available to everyone: *Does not wisdom call, and understanding lift up her voice?* (Proverbs 8:1) He tells us that wisdom requires some looking, but it will emerge if you really search.

> *Make your ear attentive to wisdom, incline your heart to understanding; For if you cry for discernment, lift your voice for understanding; If you seek her as silver and search for her as for hidden treasures;* Proverbs 2:2-4

He tells us that if we have trouble knowing which is the wise course among many options, then look for the friends of wisdom. They will always cluster around the wise choice.

> *I, wisdom, dwell with prudence, and I find knowledge and discretion. The fear of the Lord is to hate evil; pride and arrogance and the evil way and the perverted mouth, I hate. Counsel is mine and sound wisdom; I am understanding, power is mine.* Proverbs 8:1, 12-14

Wisdom is out there. The path will become clear if you want to find it. Many people are so distracted by what they feel or want that they fail to push for wisdom. Leaders must push through their own selfish impulses and evaluate possible options with ruthless rigor, looking at both short-term and long-term results.

How do skilled leaders make wise decisions?

Wise decisions come from two things: first, knowing what a wise decision looks like and, second, working a proven process to find it. In other words, you have not found a wise decision unless it will meet certain outcomes and, second, it must have passed through a predictable process. There are probably other processes that consistently render wise decisions, but this one has proven its worth to many different leaders over a long span of time.

The outcome of a wise decision is always a Triple Win: God wins; others win; and you win. If one of these is missing, then it is not a wise decision. The wisest leadership decisions move through five phases and answer five questions.

The five-phase process that a decision moves through is:
- Ô **The Discussion phase** where all ideas and points of view are on the table.
- Ô **The Counsel/Information phase** where input is sought from many different sources and the five questions are beginning to be answered
- Ô **The Options phase** where everybody's options are discussed, not just the original idea.
- Ô **The Prayer phase** where God is asked and listened to in regards to this decision or direction.
- Ô **The Decision phase** where a decision is clearly being made with a little window for new input or a change, but then it is eventually made.

The five questions which must be asked and answered during the five phases are:

1) Is it Scriptural and/or ethical? In other words, does this idea or direction agree with, promote, or violate any biblical or ethical principles?

2) Am I (we) being righteously or providentially guided, directed, or prompted to move in this direction? Are there open doors and provision for this decision? Prayer/providence (Open doors, provisions, peace).

3) Do I have clearance and input from proper authorities to move in this direction? Authorities (familial – government – spiritual – vocational); play by the rules.

4) Have I gotten input from people who are wise and or experts in the field? Wise Christians and experts (general – specific in the direct area of questions).

5) Does this idea or direction make sense in some way? Common sense (spiritual, emotional, psychological, physical, work, etc.).

If you move through these questions and this process with the agreed-upon biblical outcome, then you will arrive at a wise decision. Let's take a look at this in a little more depth.

What do wise decisions look like?

Wise decisions are **TRIPLE WIN** decisions. There are three parties that must win in every wise decision: God, others, you. *The fear of the Lord is the beginning of wisdom* (Proverbs 1:7). Jesus declares that all of the Bible can be summed up in two commands. *Love the Lord your God with all your heart, soul, mind and strength and your neighbor as yourself* (Mark 12:30, 31). In these statements we can see that all truly wise decisions must produce a win or some form of love for God, others, and you. Let's go back to that diagram at the beginning. You are looking for the line of action that results in a Triple Win. There may only be one or there may be several.

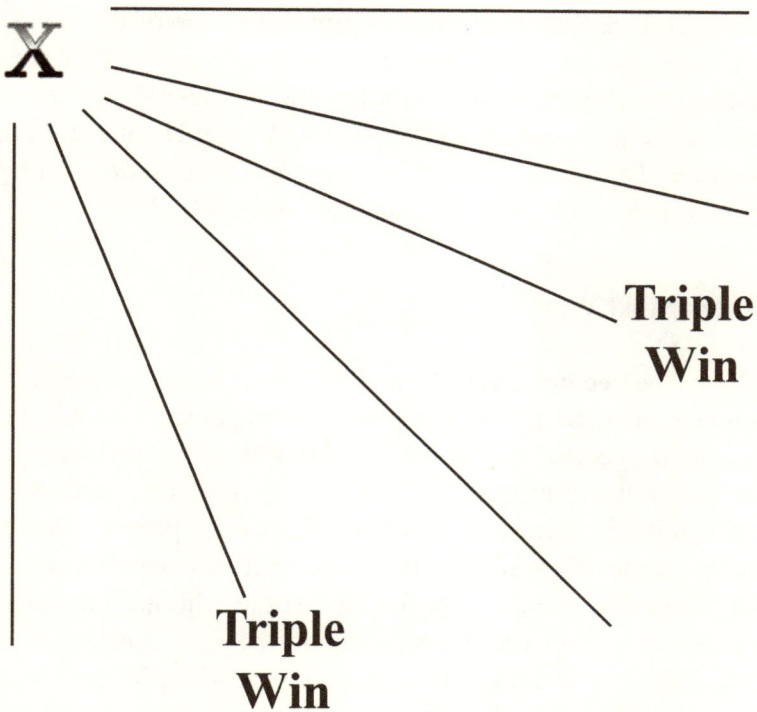

X

Triple Win

Triple Win

God Must Win

The **first part** of the triple win means that God wins. The decision must give God glory. It must not be immoral or unethical. It must conform to all we know about God and His character. It must honor God and be within His boundaries. Often times we will be presented with a desirable goal and yet the quickest or only way to get to the goal is by going outside the moral boundaries of God. We would have to lie, cheat, steal, murder, dishonor, discriminate, etc. in order to accomplish this goal. Unless you can find a way to accomplish the desirable goal without resorting to immorality or unethical behavior, it is not a wise decision to proceed.

The shortcuts of immorality and unethical behavior will always present themselves as easy ways to accomplish a good purpose. But they rob wise decisions of God's blessing and they never produce the reward that is promised. One of the basic tenets of a civilized society is that there are some things that we could do that we should not do. Finding the Triple-Win decision must involve the pleasure of God by staying within His moral boundary structure. The Bible states that, *There are ways that seem right to man but it is truly a way of death* (Proverbs 14:12).

Others Must Win

The **second part** of the Triple Win is that others must win in a wise decision. The other people impacted by this decision must gain in some way. A wise decision does not produce gain for one individual at others' expense. Every righteous party wins in a wise decision. Decisions always affect other people. The people whom the decision affects must win or the decision is not a wise one. There has to be a way for the people who are impacted by a decision to win or the decision cannot be wise. One should walk away from any direction where the only people who benefit are the deciders themselves. Leaders can be tempted to pursue personal gain and the selfish win, but that is not a wise decision.

Too often business leaders, political leaders, and even church leaders have not thought about how the people under them will be impacted by the decisions that they make. The wise direction will not always be the win that is the easiest to embrace. There may be layoffs. There will be hard conversations. There may be promotions given to others. But there is a way for the person to win even in these hard decisions. It is this "others win" that often takes the longest time to find. Keep searching; it is there.

Many times the win becomes obvious when the people affected are brought into the process. They may have completely different ideas about what a win looks like. Reality needs to be shared and the various scenarios explored.

Ask yourself the following questions:
Ô   How does the staff win if I make this decision?
Ô   How does my spouse win if I make this decision?
Ô   How does my family win if I make this decision?
Ô   How do my colleagues win if I make this decision?
Ô   How does my community and/or neighbors win if I make this decision?

Too often we only ask the question: "How do I win if I make this decision?" This is a valid part of the decision making process, but it is not the only question you should ask and answer. Remember, stepping on people to stand taller is not a winning strategy for life. Even if you get to the top, you are all alone and no one under you respects you or likes you.

You Must Win

The **third part** of the Triple-Win decision is that you must win. Unfortunately some people have thought that they must lose or "sacrifice" if a decision is godly. Many times there is a "sacrifice" of short-term gain or sinful gain for long-term gain or relational gain. Wise decisions involve a personal win, not a loss. There must be some kind of win for the individual in every wise decision or it is not a wise decision. There are all kinds of ways to win and you must construct the path, the goal, and the process so that you gain in some meaningful way or you won't stay at the task. There must be some personal gain. I have watched people who believe that the only altruistic way to be is to personally sacrifice for the good of others. But this eventually is a self-defeating proposition. Scripture does not demand this martyr point of view but instead points out subtler and deeper forms of winning.

When you are working towards a decision or goal, the wise ones will always have the component of some type of personal meaningful win. It may be a relational win versus a monetary win. It may be an eternal win versus an egoistic win. It may be an internal win versus a popularity win.

The Wicked Can Lose

A word of caution and balance: there is a group that can and should lose – the wicked. Much has been made recently about how everyone should win in good decisions. This is a wonderful idea, but it is naïve about the true nature of the world. The Bible clearly says that we live in a broken and sinful world (Romans 3:23) where some people have completely turned to moral evil. Therefore, there is often a fourth party affected by wise and unwise decisions – the wicked. The wicked are those who are consistently immoral, oppressive, selfish, and unethical in their means or ends. This group will often lose when truly wise decisions are implemented. So it is naïve to say that everybody wins in a good decision. If there is a group in a decision outcome who consistently pursue immoral, oppressive, selfish, or unethical methods of objectives then this group should lose. This group is always invited into the win of a wise decision by abandoning their rapacious selfishness and oppressive behavior; but if they do not change methods and goals, then this group should lose. Yes, the wicked can be given the chance to repent and share in the win but only if they give up their wickedness. One does not play win–win scenarios with Hitler.

Triple-Win Exercises

List three decisions that you have to make within the next month. Choose possible decisions in each case which fulfills the three criteria: God wins, others win, you win.

1.

2.

3.

What is a Proven Process to Arrive at a Wise Decision?

A wise decision answers five sets of questions and moves through five phases. Wise decisions are a process not usually a bolt from the heavens. One of the things I must regularly do with myself and with many others is slow down the decision making process. What seems right at the beginning may not be the right or wise decision when enough examination has been done. There may be other processes, but the process discussed in this book has proven itself. Work this process for your major decisions and you will see God's will unfold for you.

What is the five- phase process that a decision moves through?

1. **Discussion phase** where all ideas and points of view are on the table.
2. **Counsel/Information phase** where input is sought from many different sources and the five questions are beginning to be answered. This is often where many of the questions from the five questions are answered.

3. **Options phase** where other options and solutions to the problem are discussed, not just the original idea.
4. **Prayer phase** where God is asked and listened to in regards to this decision or direction. This is another look at the second question. Is God guiding or providentially providing for me in a certain direction?
5. **Decision phase** where a decision is clearly being made with a little window for new input or a change, but then it is eventually made.

Wise decisions take time; they are rarely instantaneously available. Bad decisions are impulsive, selfish, and destructive. In order to avoid bad decisions, one must embrace a truth about wise decisions. Wise decisions are a process. The process may have occurred in the past which allows a wise decision to emerge rather quickly, but all wise decisions are a process. If leaders are going to overcome the seduction to make an impulsive decision, then they must slow down their final decision so that they can be sure it is wise.

Everyone fears impulsive decisions. Employees fear that their bosses will impulsively or selfishly make decisions that will sideline their career or lay them off. Children fear that their parents will impulsively and selfishly make decisions to deny their fun, or more seriously, to move or break up. Christians fear that their church leaders will quickly or destructively change a cherished aspect of their church. Husbands and wives fear that their spouse will impulsively damage the finances, the relationship, or their children. Everyone benefits from wise decisions rather than selfish and/or impulsive ones, but few people are willing to put in the time to go after wise ones. This is why Solomon, in the Proverbs, says that wisdom must be searched for as if for silver.

Wiser, older leaders have learned to have some kind of process that slows down the rash "It sounds good to me!" thinking that they had in their young years. Those leaders who survive in high positions of authority over time do not make major decisions quickly or with no thought. Even if a wise leader makes a decision quickly, the quickness of that decision usually comes out of a heritage of previous experiences and information that allows them to bring out a gem of a decision quickly.

We have already seen that wise decisions benefit God, others, and you. In order to arrive at this kind of decision and find the actions, words, or goals that are wise, I have found the following process to be very helpful. **First**, a discussion phase – where an idea can be explored by people who will not immediately condemn it; **second**, a counsel/information phase – where research, analysis, and the five questions are used to test the idea; **third**, an options phase – where other options are discussed as well as additions, changes, and alterations to the original idea are made and discussed; **fourth**, a prayer phase – where God is asked and listened to regarding the idea and the other options; and **fifth** and finally a decision phase – where the right decision begins to emerge and you need to move in that direction

This chapter will be showing the wise decision process so that you can understand it and incorporate it in your life. Once this five-step process has been mastered, wise decisions can be made much quicker. Learn the process and grow in your ability to make wise decisions. Those who follow you will grow in their appreciation of your leadership when they see consistently well thought out and wise decisions flowing out of your leadership.

It is important to realize that the phases of a decision are the time to ask questions of an idea and evaluate whether it should be pursued or not. Not all good ideas should be pursued for any number of reasons.

Idea Phase

This is where a new idea is birthed. This may happen in the mind of a single individual or it may happen in a brainstorming session with a number of people. It is important to not judge or evaluate ideas in this phase. Great ideas can be killed too early by evaluating them in this initial part. The rest of the process is dependent upon what happens in this phase. You must have a wise idea for it to handle the rigors of evaluation.

The Discussion Phase

First, when a possible idea, direction, or goal presents itself, some kind of discussion is needed. All the relevant partners should be a part of at least one, if not more, discussions about the idea or issue. One cannot just decide whether they like the idea and then move forward. The idea must be looked at from a number of different angles, like a chess piece who has been moved to a possible new position but one does not remove their finger.

Ô I was thinking about doing this?

Ô I was at a seminar and they suggested that_____works better; should we change?

Ô It sounds like the wave of the future is_____; should we change?

Ô You know the problem we have had with_____. I was wondering what you think about our doing _____ to solve that problem?

Ô What changes if we do this?

Ô What are the probable results if we do this?

Ô Who benefits if we do this?

Ô Who is harmed if we do this?

Ô Ideas can be discarded, changed, or killed in this phase; but this phase is typically more positive. How could this work? You are still trying to ask and answer the five questions but usually from the positive angle.

The Information/Counsel Phase

After a discussion phase (sometimes during), a second phase opens up called the counsel/information phase. This is when there is a need for facts, input, alternative perspectives, legalities, and past experiences. This phase may take quite a bit of time to collect the crucial information so that an informed decision can be made. This phase may involve calling experts and wise people from across the country. It will certainly require conversations with bosses, authorities, and key decision makers in regard to their attitude toward the idea. Who should we talk to in order to gain wisdom regarding this new idea? What facts should we get a hold of to know if this is a good thing? What research should we conduct to get a more definitive answer about this idea or direction? Who should we ask to study this so that we have clearer perspectives on this? It is the answers to these questions and the discussions that you have with other leaders that expand your thinking and give critical insights. Many times the idea that you originally had will not work for some reason but combining it with some other good ideas is a home run. But you have to go through the various phases to combine the various ideas.

During this information/counsel phase, the leader is really trying to answer the five questions.

1. Is it Scriptural and/or ethical?
2. Am I being guided or providentially led in a particular direction?
3. Do I have clearance and input from the appropriate authorities about this idea?
4. Have I received input from experts on this idea and wise individuals with proven success?
5. Does this idea make sense on some level or in some way?

The answers to these questions are crucial to determining whether God is giving you the green light to move forward because this is His will. Let's take a look at these questions in a little more detail.

Is it Scriptural and/or ethical?

The Bible has many commandments and principles scattered through its pages. The first issue in regards to Scripture and ethics is the outcome question. Does this idea or direction result in a Triple Win? How does God win? How do others win? How do I win? Is there some way that this first principle of wisdom and Scripture be met? If this idea or direction seems to promote this outcome, then it is a good sign to continue moving forward. If the idea clearly needs some kind of tweak to result in a triple win, then it is already time to move to options.

Remember that the implementation of any idea will require lots of details and processes. Some questions need to be asked about the implementation and their agreement with Scriptural principles. There are biblical principles that guide and bring boundaries to all of life.

Am I (we) being righteously or providentially guided, directed, or prompted to move in this direction?

At various points – especially in a Christian organization – the leader or leaders will get an idea or direction that needs to be checked out as potentially from God. Just because a person thinks it might be from God does not make it so. This whole process is about checking out an idea. Is this just an idea that floated through my head or is it God directed? God works through providence: the providing of open doors, resources, and timing. All of these things can and should be explored. God is not offended if a person tests to see if they actually did hear from God. (1 John 4:1-5; Acts 16:9, 10; 1 Thessalonians 5:16-22).

Many use the idea of receiving peace when they pray about a particular direction or idea. This may or may not be from God, but it cannot be the only evidence that God is guiding you to a particular direction. If God is directing in a particular direction, then there will be more than just one prompting. There will be confirming evidence and encouragement. It is reasonable to ask God in prayer to make it clearer. The path of the Lord becomes clearer and clearer (even if it is difficult) the more one moves in that direction. So ask yourself and others: do we have confirming evidence that God is moving us in this direction?

Do I have clearance and input from proper authorities to move in this direction?

Most people do not like to confirm with authorities an idea or direction. But most wise leaders have learned the hard way that this question cannot be ignored. Everyone has authorities in their life whether they like it or not (God, governmental, spouse, vocational, spiritual). The following questions should be asked and answered during this third phase. What is required to meet legal requirements in regards to this idea? What does my boss think about this idea? Have I run this past those who know the Bible better than I do? Is there some Scriptural principle that I may be missing? How does my spouse feel about my implementing this idea? What impact will this idea have on my family?

A number of times people think they know what the various authorities will say and, therefore, do not bring it to them. This is usually a mistake because you may be surprised by those in authority in your life. Their suggested tweaks to an idea may be the exact changes needed to make it work. The relationship that is built through bringing them the idea will help all other aspects of your life.

Have I gotten input from people who are wise and/or experts in the field?

One of the most consistently helpful steps in any decision making process is asking those who have lived a wise life and those who are experts in the area you are looking at venturing into. Make the calls, the appointments, and have the discussions with these people. They will be honored by your request for their wisdom and you will hear new ideas and combinations of ideas that you may never have thought of.

Most ideas are about a particular arena that has a body of knowledge and there are people who know that arena very well. Take the trouble to make those calls. These experts may be formal experts by virtue of their education or informal experts by virtue of their success. Ask them for their help in evaluating an idea. Sometimes they will be able to tell you about how many other people have come up with that idea and failed. Other times they will encourage a new direction because of its promising results in another situation.

You never know what you will hear from experts and the wise, so ask the questions, ask for advice, and take notes on their responses. It is the foolish leader who only consults himself and those who have to applaud their ideas.

Does this idea or direction make sense in some way?

All good ideas will make sense in some way. Most of the time one is evaluating an idea in terms of common sense. Will this produce the desired result for the individual or the ministry? If it will, then it at least meets the common sense question. I have run across leaders who are trying to do things that make little or no sense except for the ego sense it makes to them. Ask yourself whether an idea or direction makes common sense. And ask other people if they can also see this path as a good one.

There are other times when an idea or prompting seems to not make sense, but it is the right thing to do. This is where an idea makes sense in a different way: spiritually, financially, emotionally, psychologically, physically, etc. There are ideas that spiritually make sense but naturally seem idiotic. An example would be Abraham believing he would have a son through Sarah even though both were well past eighty. There are ideas that make perfect psychological sense but little else. An example would be Solomon's order to have a baby chopped in two and half distributed to each woman claiming to be its mother. There are times when things make spiritual sense but little financial sense like when Scripture suggests that people give a tenth of what they earn back to the Lord's work as an act of worship. This makes no financial sense, but it does make perfect spiritual sense (Proverbs 3:9,10). I have on occasions suggested an abuse victim confront directly the person who abused them (in a safe environment). This is very difficult and makes no sense on one level, but often it makes all the difference in their healing.

The Options Phase

As the information/counsel phase continues, nears completion, or is completed, a third phase opens called the options phase. This is where the original idea is tweaked in some way or combined with another idea. This could also be where the original idea is completely abandoned and a new or even opposite idea is pursued because of the previous phases. Are their options or modifications to this idea which are more beneficial? What are the various options regarding this idea, direction, or goal? A willingness to listen to modifications to the original idea often results in great innovation and benefit. If this idea is coming from someone else, what need/desire are they aiming at meeting through this idea? Is it a good idea but a bad plan to accomplish it? Is there a better way of meeting the need? Is something hidden in this idea that could be damaging or brilliant?

The Prayer Phase

After the various options have been thoroughly explored, a fourth phase takes front and center that hopefully has been going on all along – this is the prayer phase. This is where you actually take the time to submit the various options to God in prayer. The process of discussing the ideas with God and listening for His guidance is crucial and often neglected. One must be comfortable in your soul that a new direction will not offend God but also pleases Him. Leaders must be comfortable letting some time go by after prayer and not rushing to the decision phases. For prayer to work effectively, you must listen for the answer to your times of prayer. Prayer must not be a perfunctory process with little expected of it.

The Decision Phase

The final phase of a wise decision is called the decision phase. This is where the leader lets the key people know that a decision is about to be made. A decision has not been made at the start of this process but the leader is leaning in the direction of a particular decision as that seems the best course of action. This gives the other people a chance to add any new facts or to make any new appeals before the final decision is rendered. As you can tell from the above description, wise decisions don't just happen – they are sought after, mined, and pursued.

Wisdom Process Exercises

Ô Make little cards with each of these phases of a good decision on it and explain the process to your board, spouse, or committee. Begin working through an idea using this process.
  o Idea Phase
  o Discussion Phase
  o Counsel/Information Phase
  o Options Phase
  o Prayer Phase
  o Decision Phase

Make a chart with the five phases of the wisdom process across the top and room for some notes below each phase. Make one of these charts for five different ideas that you are working through or would like to work on. Chart your progress on each discussion. Decision is listed twice.

Idea, Decision, Goal	Discussion	Counsel/ Information	Options	Prayer	Decision

- Ô Make a card with the five questions on it and carry it around in your wallet or purse.
    - o Is it Scriptural and/or ethical?
    - o Am I or the company being righteously or providentially guided, directed, or prompted to move in this direction. (open doors, provisions, peace).
    - o Do I have clearance and input from proper authorities to move in this direction? Familial – Government – Spiritual – Vocational
    - o Have I gotten input from people who are wise and or experts in the field?
    - o Does this idea or direction make sense in some way?

Conclusion

Making wise decisions is possible. It is both an art and a science. It requires a willingness to go after the right outcome, the Triple Win, because you know it exists; making wise decisions and being willing to walk away from a decision if it is only selfish and profitable. Wise decisions are not usually low hanging fruit but instead require time, different perspectives, and a process. No one is just anointed with wisdom so that they do not need to work through what they are thinking. A healthy process is needed to ensure that the triple-win choice emerges clear and distinct. When in doubt look for the eight friends of wisdom and you will be able to make a wise decision every time. Look for prudence, knowledge, discretion, the fear of the Lord, counsel, sound wisdom, understanding, and power. They will be hanging out with wisdom.

Wise Decision Making Overview

What do wise decisions look like?

The outcome of a wise decision is always a Triple Win: God wins; others win; and you win. If one of these is missing, then it is not a wise decision.

What is a proven process to arrive at a wise decision?

The wisest decisions move through six phases and answers five questions.

What is the six-phase process that a decision moves through?

1. The Idea phase: where new ideas are brought up but not evaluated.
2. The Discussion phase: where all ideas and points of view are on the table.
3. The Information/Counsel/phase: where input is sought from many different sources and the five questions are beginning to be answered.
4. The Options phase: where everybody's options are discussed, not just the original idea.
5. The Prayer phase: where God is asked and listened to in regards to this decision or direction.
6. The Decision phase: where a decision is clearly being made with a little window for new input or a change, but then it is eventually made.

What are the five sets of question?

1. Is it Scriptural and/or ethical?
2. Am I (we) being righteously or providentially guided, directed, or prompted to move in this direction?
3. Do I have clearance and input from proper authorities to move in this direction? Familial – Government – Spiritual – Vocational)
4. Have I gotten input from people who are wise and or experts in the field?
5. Does this idea or direction make sense in some way? Spiritual, emotional, psychological, physical, work, etc.

LEADERSHIP SKILL #8 - SYSTEMATIZE: EXTERNALIZE A SYSTEM AND DELEGATE
Involve Others in a System to Accomplish the Goal

After a few years of being a pastor, I was frustrated that the people in the congregation were not growing and enjoying their spiritual life. I preached, counseled, and visited but still no significant change in their spiritual life. Then I hit upon something which now, as I look back on it, is obvious; but at that time it seemed like a radical idea. I would show them how to do the spiritual exercises that I did every day. So I prepared a lesson on how to confess your sins each day. I prepared a lesson on how to listen to the prompting of the Holy Spirit throughout the day. I prepared a lesson on how to study the Bible every day. I prepared a lesson on how to meditate on the Bible throughout the day. I prepared a lesson on how to pray. I prepared a lesson on how to witness to people about the Christian faith. And, finally, I prepared a lesson on how to give generously to the Lord's work. This is what I thought of as the basics of a vibrant spiritual relationship with God. There were other spiritual exercises to share but that would come later. Each one of these was a simple single sheet of paper, but they revolutionized our church. It was a simple, doable system of spirituality that people could understand and repeat every day.

Average every-day men and women began to actually do my system for being spiritual and just like it did for me, they became spiritually alive and actively related to Jesus Christ in a vital way. They wanted to teach their children these spiritual exercises. They began to gather people around them at work during the lunch hour and show them the system that they were now using to be alive in the Spirit. I had shared my actual system for being spiritual, and it worked for other people. Then they couldn't help but want to share it with others. This episode taught me the power of writing down the system that you are actually using and teaching that instead of teaching theories, suggestions, and bits and pieces.

Every one of our lives is full of systems. A system is a regular pattern of steps that produces a predictable result. We have, over time, invented a series of systems that direct much of our daily lives. We have a system for getting ready in the morning. We have a system for our spiritual life. We have systems for our marital life. We have multiple systems at work. Pastors have systems for visiting the sick; for preparing and preaching a sermon; for counseling marital problems; for conducting board meetings; for teaching Sunday school; for leading someone to Christ; etc. Some of these systems are good, some are needlessly convoluted, and some lead to destructive results. Unfortunately, we keep doing our current systems until we really look at them or the results they produce.

Until we write down what we are actually doing step by step in our current system, it is hard to improve it, change it, or pass it on. I am amazed at how powerful it is to write down your system. Expose your system by writing it down. Then make improvements to your list of steps. Write down this new list. Start following the new list and watch your productivity and effectiveness rise. Show your list to others who could help improve your system.

The Biblical Basis of Systematization and Delegation

One of the greatest days of my life as a pastor/leader was when I realized that my job was to put other people to work. That was my job, the Bible said so. (Ephesians 4:11, 12) I had for too many years been running around like a chicken with my head cut off. Oh, the joy of this realization. I apologized to my congregation for hoarding the ministry. I stood up in front of my people that Sunday morning and told them that I now realized that my primary job as pastor-teacher of this church was to put them to work. I was going to give them the joy of being in the game. They were the primary lovers who would change their world and our community for Jesus. They were going to be trained how to love people and God more effectively. I had been wrong and I was going to stop doing the work and give it to them. I was going to encourage them and tell them everything I knew about how to do the work of God. I was going to applaud them, exhort them, and congratulate them. I finally understood what Ephesians 4:11, 12 said, *And He gave some as apostles, and some as prophets, and some as evangelists, and some as pastors and teachers, for the equipping of the saints for the work of service, to the building up of the body of Christ.*

It was right there in black and white: pastors-teachers' primary function was to equip the saints. It was not the pastor's job to do all the loving, serving, praying, counseling, etc. His job was to equip people so that they could fill their lives with love. My job was not to do the work; it was to put other people to work doing the right things. Before this I had always been the primary actor. This was the same mistake that Moses had made in his leadership. At least my failures had been made by great leaders.

Moses was one of the greatest leaders the world has ever seen. But he was a complete leadership failure on more than one occasion. Twice he tried to deliver the people all by himself. His personal discipline, work ethic, vision, and people skills were wonderful; but he failed to realize that leadership is a team sport. You can't do it well all by yourself. (Exodus 2:11-14; 18:13-27)

Leadership means causing action in the right direction. But if you are the only person acting, then your leadership has limited impact. If, however, you can get lots of people doing small pieces of the right action you can make a huge impact. In order to accomplish this kind of leadership, you must systematize and delegate effectively.

One of the consistent problems in Christian ministry today is burnout. That is often a symptom of an inability to systematize and delegate. Jesus promised that if we came to Him, we would no longer be weary and heavy laden. (Matthew 11:28) Yet many of the most overburdened and weary people I meet are Christian pastors and church workers. It is not God's will for leaders to neglect their families, their bodies, and have no life while trying to do everything for others. If the ability to systematize and delegate are not developed in the leader, there will be the predictable burnout and underdeveloped ministry.

What does it mean to systematize?

In many cases, we keep our systems secret. These action steps are treated like our trade secrets. They are what keeps us employed. Some feel if they shared their systems then they would be replaced. But in church work the exact opposite happens. The more you write down your system and delegate your systems to others, the more you are promoted. This means that you must externalize your systems, expose your systems to improvements, and help people use your systems so that the organization and the individual can succeed maximally. Sharing your system makes you a hero in church work.

A good leader helps people see a job as the accomplishing of a series of steps. Each individual brings his/her uniqueness to a system, but it is the system that accomplishes the desired results. As long as you work the system, it should produce the desired result regardless of who is doing the steps. When the system no longer produces the results, then it is time to look for a new system. Too often in church we are hiring people for their hidden system instead of their ability to involve other people in their system. The key to effective organizational leadership is involving others in successful systems. Many hands make light work. The biblical definition of a church leader is someone who equips others to do the work of service.

Let me tell you the story of a pastor we will call Pastor Bill who faithfully serves a small church. He desires to expand his ministry and reach more people for Jesus, but it never happens. He works tirelessly, but he allows people to pull him back into doing all the work himself. They praise him, applaud him, and love on him every time he prays, he visits, he preaches, and he serves, and they complain, criticize, and withhold praise every time he leads, delegates, trains, and supervises. Pastor Bill is caught in the small-church ministry cycle.

In order to get his church to grow, Pastor Bill has to do things that give him no applause. In fact, he has to do things that his church doesn't want him to do. He has to stop doing everything and force them to become the church (the active body of Christ in their community). He has to externalize his systems that they love so much so that others can be trained how to do them. People will resist this because it is easier to just pay the pastor to be spiritual for us. Externalizing a system and delegating it to others is an essential leadership skill. Without developing this skill, Pastor Bill will forever be stuck in a small ministry doing everything and reaching a very limited number of people.

One of my personal problems in pastoring a church was that I enjoyed doing the ministry too much. I enjoyed getting the late night call. I enjoyed being the only one who could counsel a couple. I enjoyed preaching and teaching five to eleven times a week. I enjoyed running the meetings. I enjoyed showing all my skills and doing my systems. However, our church kept running into the two-hundred barrier and blowing up because I was doing everything. We did not move past the two-hundred barrier until I started externalizing my systems and letting other people use them, improve them, and invent better ones. I realized that I had been hoarding all the joy of ministry for myself, and I needed to let others in on the wonder of serving God by loving others.

Having an externalized system allows everyone to understand it, improve it, and/or invent something better. In the beginning it may be intimidating to have your system written on a board for all to see. But there are a number of benefits of going through this externalizing process. This next section shows you a system for externalizing your systems.

How do we uncover and improve your current systems?

A number of years ago the church I led was not growing even though we were having a lot of visitors each week. We wrote down what we were actually doing to connect people to the church. We were doing the standard welcome in the service: a gift for coming and a letter during the week. This was resulting in twenty-three percent of our visitors connecting to the church and becoming regular attenders or members. Twenty-three percent is usually a good number but because of the economic situation in our community, we needed a much higher level of assimilation or we would shrink significantly. After writing down what we were doing, we suggested additional things we could do to make people feel welcome; and we looked at what other churches were doing to assimilate people. After much discussion and interaction, we added twelve other steps to what we were doing. This is what we ended up doing:

Ô We put people in the parking lot to greet people as they were walking to the church.
Ô We put an information table out in front of the front door.
Ô We put greeters out in front of the front door of the church.
Ô We added hosts and hostesses to welcome people personally to each section of the auditorium.
Ô We offered people tours of the children and teen area before service started.

Ô   We welcomed them in the service.

Ô   We gave them a gift in the service.

Ô   We thanked them for coming as they left the service and went to their car.

Ô   We dropped a gift by their house to express our thanks for visiting our church.

Ô   The Senior Pastor called the people Sunday or Monday evening to thank them for visiting and answer any questions they might have.

Ô   We sent them a pastoral letter during the week letting them know how we could serve them and all the various programs and opportunities at the church.

Ô   We had a staff person call them on the second Sunday after their first visit to explain that area of ministry. We picked a person who most likely would correspond to their area of interest.

Ô   We sent them a church letter about the program or ministry area that they were the most interested in.

Ô   We would send letters and make calls inviting them to the church orientation classes that were coming up. (Foundations, Christian Maturity, Baptism, Service, Membership)

Ô   We would phone and send a letter to invite them to a Newcomers' Dessert at the pastor's home. This took place once a quarter at the beginning and then once a month after a while.

Our retention of new visitors skyrocketed to eight-two percent. Our church stopped shrinking and started growing. This would never have happened if we had not really looked at the inadequate system we were using to retain visitors.

Remember, you are currently using some kind of a system to do everything that you are doing. The only question is whether it is the best system for accomplishing the task and is the best system for you. We all get comfortable with our way of doing things. And it is very uncomfortable to change systems or add new steps, but often we must. Learning and growing involves adopting parts of or all of other people's systems. It is possible for anyone at any age to learn a new system. The goal is a better outcome, not preserving your old system.

The following is an essential improvement process. Examine your current system. Add to the current system. Look for other more effective systems. Confirm the results of your current system. Changes systems if you are not getting the results you want.

Step 1: Write down your systems for accomplishing the various assignments in an area of ministry: how do you do evangelism; how do you select, prepare, and deliver the sermon; how does the church connect new people to the church; how is the bulletin prepared and delivered; how does the church visit the sick; how are the preparation and flow of board meetings determined; what happens when a person comes in for marital counseling; how are Sunday school teachers recruited, selected, and trained, etc.

It is very crucial that you actually write it down or diagram it on a piece of paper. In this way you can get it outside of yourself and examine it. It is not the same to just think about it or talk about it. Many of the shortcomings of your present system will not become apparent until it is objectively clear what you are doing.

Step 2: Prayerfully examine your current system. Sometimes it is obvious that there are ways to improve your current system. If there is no prayer or publicity for an upcoming evangelistic event, you have missed a crucial step. Sometimes the system you have instituted is not what you are actually doing and this is the breakdown in the system. Phone calls to the children who did not attend that week is great, but no one is actually making the calls. Sometimes you are doing your system well, but times have changed and a whole new method is needed to accomplish the same result. We do not want to be using flannel graphs to explain Bible stories in a DVD world. If you can see where your current system is incomplete, then add those new steps into the system. Making a phone call to visitors within forty-eight hours and thanking them for their visit made a huge difference in visitor retention.

Step 3: Show your system to other people and ask for their input on how to make it better. Some of the best staff meetings you will ever have are when you get everyone's brains to focus on improving an incomplete church system. There are all kinds of different people who will provide tons of insights for improving your current system.

Step 4: Look at various other systems for accomplishing the goal. Sometimes you can incorporate other aspects of other people's system. Sometimes you need to scrap what you are doing and adopt someone else's system.

I regularly run across pastors who want to keep developing sermons the way that is comfortable for them – the way that they learned in seminary – even though it is no longer effective or has stagnated in terms of the number of people that method will reach. I often have to introduce people to video clips, sermon illustration services, research teams, and new styles of delivering biblical content. If a person will not grow in their communication of the Bible, they can only reach the people who like that style – or worse yet – people who like them.

Step 5: Hire someone to run your improved system or someone who has an effective system of their own. Let me give you an illustration. At a critical point in our church's history, I hired Pastor Jim to come on staff and help us in children's ministry. We didn't realize Pastor Jim had a much better system for children's ministry than we had ever seen before. Children's ministry was always a hodgepodge of teachers, last-minute appeals, and thrown-together lessons. But within a few short months, Pastor Jim had children's ministry running like a fine Swiss watch. The ministry was growing and expanding beyond anything we had seen before.

He had a system and it was clearly working. I remember sitting down with him and asking him what he was doing and why it was working so well. He drew out on a piece of paper showing the system he was using with all its parts, interactions, and expansion capabilities. It was brilliant and was clearly working.

I realized a number of things after we hired Pastor Jim. First, I was no good at children's ministry. Second, I didn't have the best system in various arenas of the church. Third, there were people who had much better systems and I should let them do it, unhindered. Fourth, if our church was going to grow, I needed to hire more people like Pastor Jim to deploy effective systems in every area of the church. Fifth, in order for more people to be involved effectively in church, the leader must have a system and be able to involve others in it.

Leadership Exercise

Ô   Pick an aspect of your ministry and write down your system for doing it.
   o   Let other people see it and comment on it.
   o   Add new steps as needed.
   o   If the key leader does this, then others will be willing to do this.

How do you delegate effectively?

One of the questions that regularly comes up in churches and other volunteer organizations is how do you get people in the church to do parts of the ministry? The answer to that is you delegate to them a system so they do not have to invent what they are doing as they go along. People feel much more inclined to accept a responsibility if it is clear what is expected of them. Once a person has mastered the basic system, then their creativity can add to the system or change it.

Step 1: List the outcome to be achieved, the results wanted, the goal desired, the win

It is very important that the outcome be established. This is important because the volunteer may have a much better system to achieve the objective. But they must understand what is really trying to be accomplished. As you are explaining the job to a volunteer, you might say something like

"Here is what we are trying to accomplish."
"This is what a win looks like."
"I will be very excited if these things happen."
"These are the needs that must be met by this position."

The leader needs to understand the goal before they see the system that you have put in place. If they do not see the system, then they may believe that the system is the king rather than the needs, goals, and/or outcome. There may be times when they need to deviate from the system to meet the needs of the people who come for ministry. One of the most frustrating things in the world is to try and work with a person who has elevated the system to first position over the people. The person that you have recruited or employed to do a task may have a system or an idea that will achieve the desired results more effectively. Give them the opportunity to be clued into the big picture by defining what you are really going after by this position.

In the case of a major ministry like children's, youth, weekend service, and adults, the ultimate goal of these services is going to be one of the purposes of the church: evangelism, discipleship, worship, compassion, and/or fellowship. Therefore the activities that are being done should accomplish one or more of these results. If an activity is fun but does not accomplish these goals, then it must be redesigned. We are not playing church to do what we like; we are trying to accomplish Jesus' goals.

Step 2: List out what needs to be done to accomplish that goal

This is where you write down the system you have used or you would use to accomplish the goal. These systems should have four to eight steps or key actions that the person must perform to be successful. There may be many things that they can do, but what are the four to eight actions the person should take to receive praise for a job well done. It is this little system and its goal that you are going to delegate to someone else.

Yes, there are times when it is best to delegate with no system and you are asking for the person to invent success in an area or overhaul what is being done. But most of the time delegation involves asking someone to do or improve an existing system. The key is to let the person know what are the crucial actions that will bring success. Don't leave them in the dark about how to do well.

"If you do these things, I will be very pleased."
"If you focus on doing these steps, then more people will grow in the faith."
"If you make sure that these are done, then the rest will take care of itself."

In order to accomplish a goal, certain things must be accomplished well for that goal to be reached in the right way.

The classic illustration of delegation using this idea is from the movie *Apollo 13* where the astronauts are running out of air because they have the wrong kind of CO_2 filters. The engineers on the ground have to construct a way to make square filters work in round holes using only materials that were on board the space ship. When they had figured out how to do it, they had to write down a procedure that could be radioed to the astronauts so they could duplicate the same device.

Let me give you some examples of these steps for various jobs around the church. You will immediately see that these are not complicated. This basic system makes the job delegate-able. People who have gifts in these areas can immediately see ways to improve on these basic systems, but almost anyone can do these steps.

Sample Systems for Ministry

Assimilation system for following up visitors
- Ô Greeters in parking lot
- Ô Information table
- Ô Greeters at front door
- Ô Host and hostess
- Ô Gift in the service
- Ô Pastor phone call
- Ô Gift drop by
- Ô Letter
- Ô Staff phone call
- Ô Specific info mailing
- Ô Newcomers' Brunch invites
- Ô Newcomers' Brunch

Five actions of a good greeter
- Ô Smile
- Ô Say "Hello"
- Ô Offer your name first
- Ô Extend your hand
- Ô Ask F.O.R. questions

- Ò Family: Is this your family? Do you live around here?
- Ò Occupation: What do you do for a living?
- Ò Religion: How long have you been worshipping at Twin Lakes?

Seven actions of a good usher

- Ô Smile
- Ô Look people in the eye
- Ô Extend a bulletin
- Ô Say "Hello, welcome to Twin Lakes"
- Ô Offer to find them a seat: "May I find you a seat?"
- Ô Tell parents with small children that there is a nursery and offer to escort them
- Ô During the service, *immediately* approach a mother with a fussy baby and suggest that she go to the nursery

Four keys of a good hospital visit

- Ô A Look: Make good eye contact with the person and ask them questions.
- Ô A Word: Open the Bible, read it, and give them a word of encouragement.
- Ô A Touch: Hold their hand or arm especially when you pray.
- Ô A Prayer: Pray for them. Listen to what God would have you pray.

Step 3: Demonstrate the work being done – either by you or by someone else – while they watch

Good delegation involves having the person watch someone with experience do the job. Many people learn best by imitation of a good model. The person has the list of what makes a person successful at the particular assignment and then they get to watch someone actually flesh out what is being asked. Usually this causes a person to say, "I can do this." The more involved the job, the longer the person watches or shadows the experienced person.

Far too often in church work there is too much of a rush for this step. We throw people into an assignment because we need a warm body. They have the curriculum; they have the list of things that need to be done so throw them into it. This is usually a long-term mistake. Even if a person is capable of reading and following directions, it helps to have a person do the job right in front of their eyes.

All of us have been to restaurants where we were waited on by two waitresses. The trainee is watching the experienced waitress do her thing. Usually the trainee is asked to do some small part of the job like get drinks or check how everyone likes the food. This same process is needed in church work. Give people confidence before you hand over the whole assignment to them. Too often in church work delegation is abdication.

Step 4: Ask them to do the list while you watch

When the person has watched once or twice, it is time to have them do the job and have you watch. They will not do it as well as you, but they need to get their hands dirty and do the assignment. Again we have all experienced the trainee waitress take our order with the experienced person standing behind her offering assistance if it is needed. Take the time to have someone watch people during their first time doing an assignment.

In more and more churches this is called a first-serve opportunity. And the first-serve process includes all the steps 1-4. When someone signs up to help in a ministry the leaders of that ministry know that it is a first-serve interaction, and so they do not try and load too much on or do it too quickly. There is a needed level of comfort and familiarity with a particular job before people feel at ease. Be willing to do fewer things in order to give people time to be comfortable with the assignment they are asked to do.

Step 5: Ask them to do the system that you have laid out

There is a need for the person to focus on the simple success steps of the system. Too often these get left behind after the first few months. Have one-minute meetings weekly to go over the list and focus on a particular step. Too often we have too many meetings that take too long and many of these can be eliminated if we shorten them to a minute and focus on the list.

It made a huge difference in our ushers to have seven simple steps to focus on. A sixty-second meeting was all that was needed to go over the list and emphasize one of the steps. The ushers were more confident of what they were doing. They were more focused on doing the key activities of a good usher because each week the seven actions of a good usher were emphasized.

Step 6: Ask them to improve the list, change the list, or maintain the list

By this point a person is comfortable with the various parts of the system and their importance for the whole, and now it is time to get their suggestions and new ideas. Some people will offer their new ideas and others need to be asked. Don't assume just because the person is not offering changes that they do not have any. Many times people want to change the system before they have really done it. Until the old system has been mastered, the importance of the various steps is sometimes overlooked.

The director of our Vacation Bible School one year had been a participant before and was able to make wonderful suggestions so that we had the best outreach we had ever had up to that point. Her expertise and familiarity with the current system told her where changes were needed. She instituted new positions, involved herself in new ways of recruiting, and used people in different ways. It was not a complete change from the old way that our church had done VBS, but there were significant changes.

Leadership for a Change Exercises

Ô Write down the various assignments and/or jobs in your area(s) of ministry.

Ô Write down your system for each of the assignments and jobs in your area. If there is another person who is over a sub-section of these assignments, make sure that they are included in the development of any system.

Conclusion

Remember, a ministry cannot grow beyond what one person can do if you do not externalize your system and delegate parts of the ministry to other people. The job of effective church leaders is to equip people to do the ministry. Ministry is incredibly enjoyable and wonderfully rewarding. Don't hoard ministry because you like it and it gives you great joy. Give other people the joy of changing lives in church. Allow people to experience the satisfaction of serving Jesus. Do not rob regular people of the joy of ministry by doing it all. Once a leader has identified a system that will work for a task, then they can delegate that list of steps to someone who could do it.

I am constantly on the lookout for successful systems that will result in more evangelism, more discipleship, more worship, more compassion, and more fellowship. God is directing people all over the Christian world to develop systems that work better than the ones we are currently using. We need to pay attention. Remember that in the early part of the 1700's a man named Robert Rakes invented a system of evangelizing and discipling called Sunday School which resulted in thousands upon thousands of people coming to faith in Christ and growing up in Him. Sunday School is not in the Bible; it is just a system that has worked for over three-hundred years now.

LEADERSHIP SKILL #9 - FINANCES: RAISE AND STEWARD THE RESOURCES

A number of years ago the theologian, R.C. Sproul, asked a group of pastors, "How much does it cost to do a hundred dollars worth of ministry?" The pastors thought and discussed and felt that they were being asked a trick question. R.C. exclaimed that the difficulty with this question was one of the problems with ministry types. The answer he bellowed was, "It cost $100 to do a hundred dollars worth of ministry." He explained, "Pastors were consistently trying to do a hundred dollars worth of ministry for $50 or less." Pastors need to accept the fact that they will need to raise $100 to do 100 dollars worth of ministry. Too often pastors are uncomfortable talking about money and asking for it. But raising money is a part of the job of being a leader in ministry.

Pastors who want to be fully equipped leaders must learn how to raise money and become comfortable with the process. Raising money will be a constant part of doing ministry. Luis Palau, the world famous evangelist, told the author that fifty percent of his time is spent raising money so that he can spend the other fifty percent preaching the gospel. He said that all kinds of young men come to him and ask about becoming evangelists. One of his first questions is, "Are you willing to spend fifty percent of your time asking people for money?" If you are not, then you are not prepared to be an evangelist.

Pastors who are leaders in effective ministry become comfortable with the idea that they must partner with others who have money to accomplish God's will. They must ask people to partner with them to do God's work. God has given some people the money and some people he has given the ministry calling. If they do not partner together, God's kingdom work is not expanded. If God is using you to change people's lives and eternal destinies, then people will want to partner with God by giving you money and resources. You need to know how to receive those gifts, ask for more, manage what is given, and give to other ministries as well. Good ministry leaders grow in their ability to raise, manage, spend, and give away money.

Asking for money is one half of what I call the Big Ask. The other half is asking people to give their time for ministry projects. Pastors who are going to be successful at ministry are going to have to become increasingly comfortable with asking people for their involvement and their money. Growing ministries involves more and more people getting involved and more dollars being spent. In terms of asking for money – if you do not believe in what you are doing enough to ask people for their money, then you don't believe in it enough. Your ministry must be so compelling and doing such a significant work that you believe that it is worth it for people to sacrifice good things, fun things, and even some essential things to fund it.

Many pastors are timid and apologetic about the needs of their ministry. And yet they are engaged in one of the greatest enterprises in the world. It takes money, time, and energy to bring hope to the world. The Apostle Paul's admonition to young Timothy is appropriate here. 2 Timothy 1:7 *For God has not given us a spirit of timidity, but of power and love and discipline.* If you have legitimate needs then make them known. God has decided that He will not miracle all the ministry into existence. He wants us to be participants in His kingdom expansion. People must give money, resources, energy, and time if God's kingdom work is going to go forward in this world. The leaders of ministry must become skilled at raising money and managing it or the work of God, through that church, is blocked.

The Financial Knowledge and Actions of a Skilled Leader

What does the skilled leader of a ministry know and do in the financial arena? Let me give you a quick overview of the basic financial knowledge and actions of a ministry leader. Then I will develop them in more detail. He knows that the present and future health of the ministry will come down to tithing and offering. He knows that it is his job to educate people about generosity. He knows that tithing is a biblical concept given by God to support ministry through proportional giving. He knows that he must keep people informed about the financial state of the church. He knows that some people have excess money in their bank account and would love to invest in worthy causes. He knows that he needs to cultivate relationships with people that God has blessed with the spiritual gift of giving. He knows that he must have a compelling vision and direction for the ministry or people won't be drawn to give. He knows that he must personally ask certain people to give to God's work over and above what others give. He has practiced saying what he will say until it is natural and compelling. He knows that he must provide compelling reasons to give over and above the regular giving to this new or special project. He knows that different people will give to different projects. These are the bits of information that reside in the mind of the skilled ministry leader about how ministry is funded.

I could wish that I had been aware of this chapter when I was starting out in ministry. Then it would not have taken me ten to fifteen years to discover these crucial issues of a healthy ministry. Let's take a longer look at each of these financial leadership components.

Component #1: He knows that the present and future financial health of the ministry will come down to tithing and offering

A ministry can only go as far as resources for that ministry will permit. Ministry does not run on air. As I stated earlier, God has chosen to give humans the opportunities to be partners with Him in His program. He could have decided to do it all Himself through miracles or angels; but He uses pastors, people, their skills, and their generosity. God has decreed that the leaders of ministry must recruit both people and resources. If a leader is unwilling to do either of these uncomfortable assignments then he robs himself, robs others of the joy of assisting, and robs God of the full impact of their ministry.

Pastors expect God to supply, but they often refuse to be practical about how He will supply the necessary funds to do the ministry. The church is not a profit-making business and should not become one. The church exists on the generosity of the people who participate in that ministry. Many Christian leaders find the job of raising resources so distasteful that they permanently cripple their impact rather than learn how to raise funds for ministry. Effective leaders accept that they have to raise money in order for ministry to go forward. Raising the resources for ministry comes down to people who believe in the ministry giving regular support and special gifts. This is called tithes and offerings. In other words, pastors must ask for money if their ministry is to actually work. They must ask for people to give consistently a portion of their income, and they must occasionally ask for more to fund a project or need. The leader who wants to see their ministry succeed must do this. If you are a ministry leader, you must accept this responsibility. You must believe in the work of God enough to ask people to give their money and other resources to it. If you do not believe in it enough to do that, then it does not deserve to be funded.

A number of years ago I was attending a huge church that needed to build a new building to handle all the people who wanted to hear the dynamic young pastor. He, however, was very reluctant to talk about money. He had the staff and the lay elders make all the announcements about the new building needs. The project went nowhere. Finally he asked a wise and much older pastor what was wrong. The wise pastor told this dynamic mega-church star that he would personally have to ask people to give to the project. The pastor repented and began openly talking about the project and asking people to give so that the new building could be built. The people responded when their leader asked them and the building was built.

It does not matter whether you are Moses asking people to give some of the plunder of the Egyptians to build the tabernacle or David asking the leaders of Israel to give to the erection of the temple, or Paul asking the Corinthians to support the famine relief project in Jerusalem. Ministry costs money and someone must ask people to contribute. It helped me personally to realize that this is just the way that resources are raised for ministry. As a leader I was to pray that God would supply, and then I was to ask God's people to give generously. If a pastor is unwilling to ask for money, then they have resigned from leadership. Leaders take responsibility for the resource generation as well as the content of the teaching.

Component #2: He knows that it is his job to regularly educate people about tithing and offerings

It is not enough for the pastor/leader to talk about money when a special project demands it. The pastor must regularly educate people about the need to give generously to support ministry expenses. Most successful churches do at least two things to increase the education of the congregation on financial matters. First, they dedicate a month of Sunday mornings to teach on biblical money management every year. Usually this takes the form of a stewardship month: a series of four sermons talking about biblical principles of handling money which includes tithing and offerings. Second, successful churches have classes about financial principles of money management where people learn and practice biblical solutions with their money. This biblical information should be talked about, discussed, and acted upon in all types of settings and gatherings. The issues about biblical money management and giving are too vital to be kept quiet.

The pastor must make the case biblically for every Christian to give a portion of their income to support the Lord's work. The pastor must be clear and unapologetic in regards to the commands and benefits in the Bible in regards to giving. The pastor cannot act like he is trying to get people's money for his goals (they cannot be his goals). He must point to God's ministry of changing people's lives. There are also hundreds of other actions that churches can take that will increase the regular financial support to the ministry. One of the newest is to provide people new convenient ways to give other than just checks in the offering basket. But, overall, pastors must not shy away from preaching and teaching about money. It doesn't matter if a few people erroneously believe that you talk too much about money. An effective ministry needs financial support and, therefore, you must talk about it. Pastors would not back away from talking about prayer because people think the pastor is after too much of their time.

Component #3: He knows that tithing is a biblical concept given by God to have Christians support ministry through proportional giving

Tithing is a practice which was instituted by God to honor Him. Proportional giving to support the ongoing ministries of the work of God is decreed throughout the Bible. *Set aside in store as God has prospered you.* (1 Corinthians 16:1-3) This is mentioned and discussed in both the Old and New Testament

(Genesis 14:20; 28:22; Malachi 3:10). Tithing is a religious term for ongoing proportional support for ministry in reference to this ten percent figure. Jesus declares to the Pharisees that they tithe, which is good, but they neglect weightier things, which is bad (Matthew 23:23). Some pastors and leaders argue amount percentages but that is a red herring. The people who want to argue about the percentage usually do not want to give a proportion of their income; they want to give a fixed amount that will not in any way strain their budget or honor God. Therefore do not argue about this issue. The purpose of the tithe was to honor God (an act of worship) and to provide for the work of the ministry. The minimum amount God ever asks for in the Bible was ten percent. Christians should be told that if they want to give more than this to honor God, then they can. If someone wants to give less than ten percent, that is between them and God but God never requested less than ten percent as an adequate act of thanksgiving for providing us with the other ninety percent.

All ministries must have regular ongoing support and that support must come from somewhere. Pastors should help people realize that God has given us the chance to be involved in His kingdom program through our giving. God clearly could have done it all without us; but He counts our worship through giving as pleasing and through that giving, welcomes our real participation in changing lives. If a ministry is going to have more money to expand its impact, then more people must begin giving or the same people must give more. It is usually easier and more helpful to introduce new Christians to this principle of regular support through proportional giving than long-standing Christians who have been a part of previous denominational wars over giving.

Component #4: He knows that he must keep people informed about the financial state of the church

Pastors eat, sleep, and breathe the church. They know who is doing what and who is not doing anything. They know what projects are planned and what projects cannot be attempted. They also know the financial state of the church inside and out. What many of them forget is that most of the people in the congregation do not have any idea about what a little less in the offering plate means to the various ministries. Communication with the congregation about the basic financial state of the church is what skilled leaders know to do. Unskilled leaders moan about the lack of giving and wait until there is a huge crisis before they honestly tell the congregation what is really happening with the financial affairs.

This lack of communication, except in crisis, always comes back to bite the pastor/leader. As soon as there is a financial crisis that people are unaware of, leaders within the congregation immediately assume that the problem is a lack of leadership and so they grab for the controls of the church. In their mind it is poor leadership that has caused this crisis. Really, it is a lack of communication in many cases. The pastor/leader of a ministry must constantly keep the congregation informed of both the good and bad of the financial state of the church. He must do this in a number of different ways: congregational meetings, tithing letters, announcements, bulletin statistics, private meetings, end-of-the- year reports, etc. The process of increasing regular support for ministry involves a process of information. Information is needed because believers who are being asked to contribute to a ministry on a regular basis should be informed as to where the money is going, what it is needed for, and what could be accomplished if more came in. People who give must have utmost confidence in the leaders and the organization and how they are handling the funds that they donate.

Sometimes under-skilled pastoral leaders try and keep their church's finances secret or mysterious. This is a counterproductive leadership strategy. Throw open the shutters and let everyone know as much as possible about the church's finances. Successful churches are not secretive about their financial need and goals. People in these days are suspicious of organizations that are not open about donated monies. Sometimes salaries and certain expenses need to be grouped to keep some people from condemning a particular expenditure, but the general rule of thumb is to say as much as possible about where all the money is going. If there has been a problem or a culture of secrecy in the past, then a number of regular meetings to explain the finances may be needed. The idea is that the pastor and church leaders need to foster clear understanding of exactly what is needed to operate the ministry.

Almost every long-term pastor has a story of struggling under the weight of financial pressure in ministry and then mentioning this burden to a parishioner only to have them say, "I had no idea that this was a problem!" Then when the need was made known, money poured in to take care of the problem. Most pastors believe that their story is an isolated case or a peculiar situation. No, if people are aware of the needs of a ministry, they will give to support that ministry. The less they know, the less they give. If there is a need for a new staff person or carpet or computer, let everyone know. If it costs $10,000 to keep the lights on, let people know. When the need is clear then the dollars will be supplied. I have, for years, suggested that pastors make known what they would do with money that came in over and above the currently needed budget because people will give until those goals can be accomplished. When the information is out there, people will support it.

Component #5: He knows that some people have "excess" money in their bank account and would love to invest in worthwhile causes

This will come as a shock to over half the people in any church, but some people actually have "excess" money in their checking account. Not everyone lives paycheck to paycheck. The fact that most people do and that most pastors live this way causes them to see generosity from a limited perspective. If a person is living paycheck to paycheck that means that every dollar they receive is already spoken for before it arrives. Therefore if they give away some money to a worthwhile cause, some other need or desire or payment which was already a part of their life will have to go without. To give to the church – many people think – means that you must take something away from your life. This way of thinking denies the power of God but also ignores that thirty percent or more of the people in a congregation live within their means and have savings. When the pastor has this paycheck- to-paycheck mindset, he apologizes for asking people to give to the church because he believes that the only way for a person to give is to take something away from their life. He does not talk about the privilege of investing in God's causes. He does not see benefit to the person, only the sacrifice they are making. He asks (begs) for the crumbs and leftovers from people's money.

Everyone does not live paycheck to paycheck. There are people who have a much more biblical mindset in regards to money, and they have "excess" no matter how little they make. These people live on less than they bring in and have money to invest, save, give, and use for emergencies. They can give if there is a sufficient reason to do so. They do not have to take anything away from what they are already doing in order to give to a project or cause. It is these people that will give the most money to a new project or cause. It is these people's gifts and offerings that will amount to seventy-five percent or more of a building fund. Those pastor/leaders that are successful at funding ministry and doing powerful new projects have targeted conversations with these people who could give substantially to a worthwhile project.

Component #6: He knows that he needs to cultivate relationships with people that God has blessed with the spiritual gift of giving

Every pastor knows that in order to make ministry work, the gifts and talents of the people in the church must be identified and developed. Teachers need to be teaching, exhorters need to be exhorting, leaders need to be leading, and so forth. One of the gifts that is often overlooked is the gift of giving. People with the gift of giving are often given an ability to make lots of money so that they can give as God directs them. If a pastor or ministry leader does not develop their gift of giving, they may think that their ability to make lots of money is for their benefit exclusively. They may be plagued by the problems of riches because a spiritual authority never told them that they may have been given the gift of giving so that God's work could go forward.

The person with these gifts needs to be shown how to become a fully mature Christian and how to utilize their gifting for maximum kingdom benefit. In just the same way that the couple who has an incredible marriage should be teaching and counseling couples how to have a great marriage and thereby sharing their abundance, so the couple with abundance financially should be sharing their knowledge and abundance with others. Unfortunately many pastors often treat rich people differently – either staying away from them or treating them as if they are all-wise. Just because a person has a measure of wealth does not mean they are spiritual or even knowledgeable. All people can use godly spiritual direction to keep the main thing the main thing and to help explain what God may be doing in a person's life. If a pastor will invest in developing wealthy people into fully functional Christians, then they will often invest some of their "excess" in their ministries projects.

I have had the privilege of developing relationships with a number of people who have the gift of giving. Some were wealthy and some were generous from very little, but they needed their spiritual gift developed. My spiritual development of their gift of giving, for some, has helped them not heap up treasures to their own hurt and has allowed numerous ministries to do great work. We all must come to understand much of the prompting of God through the lens of our spiritual gift. This explains so much of what God is doing with us.

Component #7: He knows that he must have a compelling vision and direction for the ministry or people won't be drawn to give

People give to a compelling picture of the future that excites them. The average Christian has a much harder time giving to maintain the current program. A three-dimensional picture of the future communicated powerfully will draw resources and time. We all want to be a part of something that will make a difference. So the ministries and projects of the church must be presented in such a way as to highlight the difference they will make in the future. The leader who wants to be well resourced in ministry must constantly tell what the future will look like if this ministry or project succeeds. They must paint a picture of specific benefits and particular people who will be blessed, changed, renewed, and forever altered because of the step they now take.

Maintenance drains motivation. People do not give sacrificially to purchase toilet paper for the church, but they will give when the project is about changing a little girl's life. The leader must paint a picture of the future that is so real that people can touch it right now through its description. The money will be given if the picture of the future is compelling enough and God is in it.

Vision leaks. Even though a leader has cast the vision, it must be re-cast over and over again. The compelling picture of the future gets pushed aside by the business and pressures of each day. We all need to be reminded of why we are giving our time, our money, and our expertise. We need to be shown the picture of the future again and again. It is not enough to cast the vision once a year, it must be recast in different ways every month, every week, and in some cases every day. The vision must be put out there and individual people need to be asked to help it happen.

Component #8: The skilled leader knows that he must personally ask people with resources to pray and give to God's work over and above what others give

Great ministry leaders have gotten over their aversion to asking for money for the projects that God has put on their heart. It costs money to do ministry and ministry is funded through gifts. Therefore people must be asked to give. The leader who wants to have a fully-funded ministry asks people with resources to give to the ministry. This is often a test for the leader. Does he/she believe in the project enough to ask people to support it financially? The larger the amount of money that is needed, the more the asking will need to be personal and one on one.

The person with the funds needs to be convinced that the leader has done their homework on a project.

Ô   Have you really thought through all that is entailed in doing this project?
Ô   Can you answer their questions?
Ô   Why should your project get their money rather than some other group?
Ô   What level of success have you had on similar projects?

They need to know that you believe in this project. They need to see your heart in regards to this project. Regular support for ministry can be handled from the pulpit, but new projects and/ or big projects need one-on-one attention to those with significant resources.

God pressed this truth home when our church was in the midst of a building campaign. As I was praying in regards to this project, God prompted me to talk to a specific wealthy person about the project. I had a sense that I was supposed to ask for a specific amount. This type of request was completely out of character from all my pastoral training. I protested that I did not know what to say and shouldn't he just offer to give it because he knew of our need? God pressed on me that I needed to ask him and I needed to practice what I would say. I practiced for an hour and a half, asking the empty chair next to me if it would like to contribute to the church's building campaign. I tried asking in all different ways until it sounded like me. After I was ready, God prompted me to go to the bank. When I arrived, there was this man coming out of the bank. I went up to him and asked if I could speak with him for a moment. I let him know that I had been praying about our building fund and in that time of prayer, God had seemed to suggest that I ask him to donate to the building fund. I asked him if he would pray about giving to the project the specific amount God and I had discussed in prayer. He thanked me for asking him to participate in the project. Early in the next week he let me know that he had prayed, and he also felt that God wanted him to donate a significant amount to the building fund. His gift, and the way he gave, it totaled a little more than what I was prompted to ask for.

Many pastors are so reticent in asking for money that they permanently cripple their ministry. Their hearts can fill with bitterness and disappointment because the funding is never there. All they have to do is develop the skill of asking for resources to do what God has called them to do. I watch more and more pastors concoct weird schemes to make money rather than just ask God's people to give generously. The way the church expands is clear: it is relationships, vision, teaching, and the generosity of the saints.

Component #9: The skilled leader understands the three parts of raising money for ministry: a compelling vision, telling your story, and asking for individuals to help

The process of raising money is not complicated. It involves three basic steps: casting the compelling vision, telling your story, and asking for the person's help. Each of these three steps must be done for large groups, small groups, and individuals. Many pastors have not understood that the leader must personally ask the people with money to give their money to support the vision. If the pastor/leader does not believe in the vision enough to overcome his natural reluctance to asking for funds to support it, then the people with money will not give to make it happen. Yes, there will be large group and small group appeals and that will raise from twenty-five percent to fifty percent of the money. But fifty percent to seventy-five percent of the money needed to fund a large project will come from individual donors who will need to be asked personally by the leader.

Let's look at each of these in a little more detail. In order to raise money for your ministry, there must be a compelling vision. Individuals, small groups, and congregations open their wallets when a compelling picture of the future is presented that they can help create. If there is no compelling vision, then go back to the chapters on reality and vision in this book and start there. Some pastors have a vague idea of what they would like to see happen. This will not draw participation and resources. A vision is something that rallies people to a better future. It fixes problems, it gives dignity, and it benefits all different kinds of people with the ability to see what they could not see – a better future. It is not just one person's dream but everyone can grasp it, own it, and expand it. It is nearly impossible to raise money for ministry that is not compelling and is not headed to any place significant.

The second major piece of raising money for a significant project is telling the story. This is where the leader communicates the story of how he/she came to believe in this story and why it is important. This also includes the stories of individuals who will be positively impacted by doing the vision. The vision must solve problems for lots of different kinds of people problems so that it is possible to tell different stories to engage different donors. The people who will give to this project are usually sensitized to particular people (women, teens, children, the poor, the unsaved, etc.). This better future helps those particular groups that they are concerned about. The skilled leader who wants to raise funds for a project will have specific stories of how the project will help different types and kinds of people.

The third element in effective fund raising is directly asking for a person to give to the project. This is where many good pastors struggle the most. They are just not comfortable asking a person to give a large amount of money to anything. They feel like they are bothering the person. The most skilled fund raisers are not asking for money but are instead letting the person make a real difference in the world. The most skilled fund raisers are letting people do something significant with their money that will reap temporal and eternal rewards.

People with money are always looking to invest. They want to invest so that they will have more money, more impact, more significance, more power, more prestige, etc. The skilled leader is simply allowing people with money to learn about something where their goals for their money will be accomplished. The person with money is not deciding what they are going to do without if they invest in this project. They are asking themselves, "What do I gain?" if I invest in this project. The gain must be clearly spelled out. The majority of the money for a ministry project will be raised one-on-one, not in large groups. The people who will give the most are those who have the funds and who are approached individually.

Skilled leaders ask for a specific amount of money from the person. It may be a range between $50,000 and $100,000 or 1.5 million and 2 million, but it is not "whatever you feel led to give." You may get turned down, but you will be surprised at the number of times you receive what you asked for. Jesus said, *Ask and you shall receive, seek and you shall find, knock and the door will be opened to you.* (Matthew 7:7) The skilled leader shows people how they arrived at the amount that is being asked. This might involve a chart which shows that in order to accomplish the goal, "We need one person to give 1 million, two people to give $500,000 and ten people to give $100,000, and I was hoping you would be our 1 million dollar giver." Asking the person for $50,000 may mean asking God for $50,000 and then asking the person to be God's answer. Asking for a specific amount may mean giving the person three options for their involvement in this vision, with the question, "Which one sounds like the level in which you want to participate?"

Component # 10: The skilled leader knows that different people will give to different projects

Donors respond to different projects and different needs. A skilled pastor/leader realizes that there are different projects that move different people. John Maxwell, in his seminars on stewardship, makes the analogy of different pockets that open for different needs. (John Maxwell, Stewardship Seminars, 1992) Some are moved to give to buildings and expansion of facilities. Some are moved to give to children in need or to the afflicted. Some are wired to feel the call of God to give to missionaries and gospel outreach. Each of these arenas is important. The pastor/ leader allows different people to give to the projects that are in line with their own personal passions. If a person with a lot of money does not give to one project, then they might give to the next project that will come.

We read of Barnabas selling some land and donating the proceeds in the formation stages of the church, but we do not hear about him making other donations. Mary was willing to donate a family heirloom to anoint Jesus before his death and burial, but after that one extravagant gift she had no more to give.

In my personal experience, I have had one person tell me that any time I was interested in money for direct evangelism, they were interested, while another only responded to erecting of new buildings, and a third was particular interested in projects that promoted discipleship and life transformation. When I have pitched church planting to people interested in supporting Bible knowledge, there was no response.

Component #11: The skilled leader knows that there are lots of different types of resources that can be donated for the cause

A skilled pastor/leader realizes that not everyone has a stash of cash to give to the project, but they may have materials and/or unused items that they can sell or donate to the church. For some people it is just too much hassle or trouble to convert an unused item to cash, but they are willing to donate it to the church so that the ministry can utilize its value. At times the ministry can use "in kind" donations where a person donates their time, equipment, or expertise to the ministry. Many people are very willing to donate to a project if they are given creative ways to participate. The skilled pastor/leader provides the knowledge, process, and people to allow people to donate what they can. Everyone can participate in the projects of the church; we must show them how.

When Nehemiah was moved upon by God to go back and rebuild the walls of Jerusalem, he asked for the king's support as well as the support of the Jews still living in the Medo-Persian Empire. He was not too proud to receive lumber, camels, officials, wagons, gold, soldiers, and the like to make rebuilding the walls possible. Moses also asked the people to donate gifts of clothes, wood, and precious metals when it was time to build the tabernacle. The people were such willing participants that they finally had to be told to stop giving. Because the vision was compelling and the ask was clear, their generosity was overwhelming.

Conclusion

Those who would be leaders do not run away from the responsibility of raising resources. Ministry takes resources and these must be raised. God has given us the opportunity to be a part of His kingdom program through asking, giving, leading, and volunteering. Leaders get over the discomfort of talking about money. Leaders believe in the cause of the ministry so strongly that they would talk with anyone who could help them fund the important work that they are doing.

Leadership Exercise

Circle three components that need development in your life.

Ô Component #1: The skilled leader knows that the present and future financial health of the ministry will come down to tithing and offering.

Ô Component #2: The skilled leader knows that it is his job to regularly educate people about tithing and offerings.

Ô Component #3: The skilled leader knows that tithing is a biblical concept given by God to have Christians support ministry through proportional giving.

Ô Component #4: The skilled leader knows that he must keep people informed about the financial state of the church.

Ô Component #5: The skilled leader knows that some people have "excess" money in their bank account and would love to invest in worthwhile causes.

Ô Component #6: The skilled leader knows that he needs to cultivate relationships with people that God has blessed with the spiritual gift of giving.

Ô Component #7: The skilled leader knows that He must have a compelling vision and direction for the ministry or people won't be drawn to give.

Ô Component #8: The skilled leader knows that he must personally ask people with resources to pray and give to God's work over and above what others give.

Ô Component #9: The skilled leader understands the three parts of raising money for ministry: a compelling vision, telling your story, and asking for individuals to help.

Ô Component # 10: The skilled leader knows that different people will give to different projects.

Ô Component #11: The skilled leader knows that there are lots of different types of resources that can be donated.

LEADERSHIP SKILL #10 - SELF-DISCIPLINE
Strategies for Managing Your Time, Emotions, Passions, Finances, and Power

A number of years ago I had the privilege of teaching a middle-aged pastor how to lead his ministry to a new level. He had never pastored a church over eighty people. We began to talk and he began to grow in the skills of leadership. We talked about many of the concepts and skills in this book. He immediately took to it and his church began to grow. It was very encouraging to see his ministry expand past a hundred, then two hundred, then three hundred, and then past four hundred. The church and the whole town was buzzing with excitement about this church. The church members began to make plans to build a big new auditorium that would handle the growing congregation.

Then one evening I got a completely unexpected call from an associate pastor. The lead pastor had been caught and had admitted an affair with his new secretary. His leadership of this dynamic church was over. I was just flattened with grief for his wife, his family, and him. How could he have let this happen? He had failed to protect himself from the temptations that will always come to leaders. Thankfully the church was fixed on Jesus and not just this pastor, and it continued to move forward.

I talked with him sometime later and he told me that as the church grew, his leadership kept growing and yet he did not increase his personal disciplines. When he was the pastor of a four hundred plus size church, women who had never found him attractive were now noticing him. He had not prepared for that. If you are successful at learning leadership skills, your organization and influence will grow but so will the level of temptation. Do not be destroyed by your inability to stay disciplined.

Let's look at this from another angle. In order for athletes to win in the Olympics they must be highly skilled in their sport, but they must also have a high level of basic conditioning to deliver those skills. It does not matter if you are a great three-point shooter if you cannot run up and down the court; you will never get on the court to show your skill. The same is true of leadership. A leader must be able to demonstrate an increasing level of leadership skills, but they must have a high level of basic life management skills undergirding their leadership or they will be unable to effectively apply their leadership over the long haul.

I have watched great leaders in every career field become disqualified because of a lack of self-discipline. Sprinter Ben Johnson, CEO Harry Stonecipher, Pastor Ted Haggard, Governor Eliot Spitzer, and financial guru Bernie Madoff are names that will live in infamy because of their lack of self-discipline and ethical lapses. They each were gifted leaders who were disqualified from positions of power, influence, and leadership because of poor life management skills.

Many Christian leaders destroy their lives and their ministry in many foolish ways. In some cases it has been my job to understand what went wrong, remove a leader from their ministry, and help a church and a family recover. It is never easy and it is always tragic. Christian leaders are held to a higher standard. They must not give into the seductions of sin or they devastate people. A failure to take full advantage of the grace of Christ in the area of personal discipline carries heavy consequences. This chapter is designed to make sure that it does not happen to you.

Let's have an honest discussion about the dark side of leadership. Leaders must be able to say no. If you are a leader you will face increased temptations. The better leader you are, the more temptations come your way. Temptations sneak up on us almost unnoticed and offer their particular brand of comfort. It is the wise leader who sets up systems and routines to make it near impossible to give into the dark side of leadership.

I have watched leaders destroy themselves most often in seven particular arenas. These seven temptations are ego, anger/bitterness, sex/pornography, money, health, jealousy/envy, and time management. These correspond directly to the ancient list of deadly temptations called the seven deadly sins. These are Pride, Envy, Anger, Lust, Sloth, Gluttony, and Greed. These act as parasites and diseases draining away the vibrancy of faith and leadership.

The Seven Deadly Sins

The following is a quick overview of the seven deadly sins. The first seduction is pride. **Pride** is what happens when you overemphasize a job well done or self-focus. Every Christian leader must develop systems to retain a teachable spirit and an "I am only a part of what God is doing." The second seduction is envy. **Envy** is what happens when you get distracted by someone else's blessings, rewards, and benefits. Every Christian leader must develop systems to "rejoice with those who rejoice" and reap the benefits and rewards that come from their path of good works. The third seduction is anger/bitterness. **Anger** is what happens when you don't handle your expectations well. Bitterness is anger turned inward. Every Christian leader must develop systems to handle their expectations and the inevitable emotional reactions when the expectations don't happen. The fourth seduction is lust. **Lust** is what happens when you don't handle your sexual drives well.

Every Christian leader must develop systems to appropriately channel their sexual drives. The fifth seduction is sloth. **Sloth** is what happens when you don't handle your time well. Every Christian leader must develop systems to manage time effectively. The sixth seduction is gluttony. **Gluttony** is the use of food, drink, drugs, alcohol, and sex in excess and/or to hide a deeper issue that remains unresolved. Every Christian leader must develop systems to moderate the pursuit of pleasure and deal with pain, grief, disappointment, and loss. The seventh seduction is greed. **Greed** is what happens when you don't handle the love of money well. Every Christian leader must develop systems to handle the love of money.

Remember that they will always be seeking entrance into your life and leadership. They want to destroy your potential, and through well placed lies, deeply damage your relational life. Don't let them. Remain vigilant.

Self-discipline is somewhat of a misnomer. Self-discipline is a weighty burden that cannot be accomplished alone. One will always let down at some point. Therefore true self-discipline is the development of systems, relationships, and routines so that super-human vigilance is not necessary. This chapter will suggest practical systems and/or routines to keep these temptations from destroying your leadership or your life.

Pride

Pride is what happens when you overemphasize a job well done or self-focus. Leadership becomes dysfunctional when a leader begins to inordinately focus on themselves, their importance, their comfort, their fame, and their desires. Every time we do something good, it generates good feelings and a level of importance. Being humble means that we keep focused on the good things that need to be done and not focus on the good feelings. Pride, instead, focuses on the feelings of importance often oversignifying what was done.

A person is humble when they keep doing what they are supposed to do even if the results of their actions have huge impact. They feel the feelings of pride but do not allow it to keep them from doing the next good or right action. It is easy to see this in sports. One player scores a basket and then runs up the court to play defense on the next play as though all they did was what they should have done. Another player scores the basket and then dances, struts, leers, and yells to call attention to their actions. This is pride. Pride will almost always distract you or put you out of position for the next good thing you should do.

Good leaders enjoy the feelings of personal accomplishment but consistently focus on the good of the organization, the good of the individuals, and are willing to be corrected. They certainly do celebrate their accomplishments, but they do not allow that celebration to become overblown. Every Christian leader must develop systems to retain a teachable spirit.

A Christian leader needs to resist the temptation to examine how important they are (Proverbs 27:2). When a Christian leader begins to think that they are at or near the center of what God is doing, they are rendered ineffective. God will move them off the stage because He can no longer count on that person to be interested in the good above themselves. Effective leadership can be crippled by excessive vanity, self-focus, or lack of teachability.

I know of two men who suffered from an incurable case of pride. Both were highly effective in the pulpit and brilliant. Everyone could see that God was preparing to use them mightily. But they allowed their heads to be turned with how wonderful they were. Their focus was moved off of the glory of Christ and on to themselves. At one point in their rise to lasting impact, both were driven from ministry for insufferable pride and an un-correctable attitude. They are now reduced to leading very small groups instead of large organizations. To this day they have been unwilling to see that God is blocking the growth of their ministry for the sin of pride. They could not rein in their self-focus, vanity, and arrogance. One man in particular began to be more concerned with what people were thinking and saying about him than whether the ministry was changing lives and pleasing to Christ. They both stopped allowing people to correct them. One fellow made sure that his stories and illustrations about himself always put him in the best light. He became more interested in promoting himself than the cause of Christ. Both now regularly sink into depression over their small impact. They are unable to see that pride has corrupted their leadership.

What systems and routines need to be put in place to keep pride from winning?

Pick one of the following exercises and do it every day this week.

Let me suggest seven ways of winning against an overactive self-focus.
- Ô First, expand your teachable attitude. Learn something from everyone you meet.
- Ô Second, serve others without needing to be noticed. Serve your spouse, your children, the poor, your colleagues, and whomever God brings you in contact with.
- Ô Third, express your ideas more tentatively. Propose your ideas as drafts, suggestions, options, and proposals rather than finished masterpieces.
- Ô Fourth, advance the cause of Christ. Make sure that Christ's glory is number one and not your advancement.
- Ô Fifth, refuse to read your press clippings. Take your accolades and put them away. Put the trophies, letters, and plaques that trumpet your magnificence in a place you can visit when you are depressed.

Ô   Sixth, re-intensify your devotional life with God. There are hundreds of different spiritual disciplines that can help you reconnect with God at a deeper level.

Ô   Seven, seek a rebuke. The Bible says that the wise man listens to rebukes and welcomes them. Ask someone to point out an area that you could improve.

Envy

Envy is a distraction. Envy seeks to redirect your focus on to another person's blessings, rewards, and gifts. If you become focused on the blessing or fruit of another person's life, then you will become envious. You can't have their blessings without their work, pain, talents, energy, and opportunities. It all comes as a package. Do you want their pain? Do you have the talent to produce their results? Do you want to have all their relationships, their experiences, and their difficulties? Life in a sinful world is full of pain, disappointments, and injustice. Don't forget that they have hidden pain and discouragement. No life is free from pain and problems in this broken world.

God has given each person good works to perform. It is those good works that produce the benefits, blessings, rewards, and enjoyments in their life. Because each of us is naturally self-focused, we can easily notice God's gracious dealings with other people and think it would have been nice if had been us. The blessings that fall into other people's lives should be rejoiced over because they give new evidence of the love and faithfulness of God. If God has been specifically faithful, loving, and kind to that person then He will be uniquely gracious to me. My job is to stay with the righteousness that I have been asked to perform. (Ephesians 2:10)

What systems and routines need to be put in place to keep envy from winning?

Pick one of the exercises listed below and do it each day this week.

Let me suggest five ways that will allow you to push back the green monster of envy and jealousy.

Ô First, be clear about the gifts, talents, passions, and experiences that God has given you. God wants to use you maximally, not as an echo of someone else.

Ô Second, look at the whole life of the person with the blessing. Do you want all their pain, all their struggles, and the work it took to gain those blessings?

Ô Third, pray for what you truly need. God does not answer selfish rants in prayer, but He will meet our needs (James 4:1-3).

Ô Fourth, re-embrace what you already have. Spend time reconnecting with someone you already know. Do something that you have always enjoyed but gotten away from.

Ô Fifth, get away from blessings that constantly cause you to envy. If one type of blessing regularly causes you to be envious, then avoid being exposed to that good thing.

Anger

Christian leaders are not zombies with no reactions to unmet expectations. It is, however, imperative that you develop ways to control your reactions so that you don't damage people's ability to follow you or destroy a relationship. The classic passage in Scripture dealing with anger is Ephesians 4:25-31:

> *Therefore, laying aside falsehood, speak truth each one of you with his neighbor, for we are members of one another. Be angry, and yet do not sin; do not*

> *let the sun go down on your anger, and do not give the devil an opportunity. He who steals must steal no longer; but rather he must labor, performing with his own hands what is good, so that he will have <u>something</u> to share with one who has need. Let no unwholesome word proceed from your mouth, but only such <u>a word</u> as is good for edification according to the need <u>of the moment</u>, so that it will give grace to those who hear. Do not grieve the Holy Spirit of God, by whom you were sealed for the day of redemption. Let all bitterness and wrath and anger and clamor and slander be put away from you, along with all malice.*

How flexible are you? Is your strength under control? We all want certain things to happen and other things not to happen. Leaders make things happen, but they never get all that they want. That gap between what you want and what actually happens creates an emotional reaction many times called anger.

- Ô Do you have the ability to adapt when things don't go your way?
- Ô Do you have the ability to remain calm and flexible when something will never be the way you want it?
- Ô Do you know how to release that emotion?
- Ô Do you have systems that make sure that anger does not destroy your ability to be followed?

The Bible is clear, "Be angry and do not sin." Anger is a normal human emotion, but it can control your thinking and acting in such a way as to destroy your life and leadership. Anger is energy to bring about change when it is contained within normal amounts. Anger can become destructive when you don't handle your expectations well. Most anger begins with unmet or unrealistic expectations. Every Christian leader must develop systems to handle their expectations. Other people will disappoint you in all kinds of ways and in many people that produces anger. Anger is an emotional reaction to an unmet expectation. It is perfectly natural to react when something that was supposed to happen did not happen. It is also perfectly natural to expect that a leader will have developed routines, systems, and boundaries around their emotional reactions so that others are not damaged.

Bitterness happens when we turn our anger inward. When we take the energy and emotional reaction to a situation and direct it at ourselves or refuse to let it out in some way, there will be people who block our progress. Some will do it unintentionally and some will do it intentionally. But God is strong enough to overcome the accidental and scheming actions of those around us if we will process our pain (Matthew 5:4) and follow His path (Romans 8:28).

What systems and routines need to be put in place to keep anger from winning?

Pick one of the exercises listed below and do it each day this week.

Let me suggest seven ways to keep the temperature down on the hot rage of anger in your life.
- Ô First, admit you are angry. Stop denying you are upset. One of your expectations has been denied and it ticks you off. Admit you are having an emotional reaction to this situation.
- Ô Second, install an emotional clutch. There needs to be a separation between the internal you and the external you. Just because we are feeling a certain way does not mean that it should be translated into action. An emotional clutch

allows your insides to spin and roll and your outsides to remain calm.

Ô Third, delay any expression of anger. Anger is an emotion and it will subside if you give it some time. Find a way to give it that time, through taking a walk, counting to one hundred, quoting Scripture, etc.

Ô Fourth, slowly repeat Scripture phrases and verses until you are calm enough to have rational control. When you feel the impulses of anger to say something or to act out your anger, take a deep breath and just repeat Scripture (Psalm 4:4; Ephesians 4:26-31; James 1:19; Colossians 3:8; 1 Timothy 2:8; Psalm 37:8; Proverbs 19:11; Ecclesiastes 7:9).

Ô Fifth, evaluate your anger for its source. Anger is an emotional reaction to unmet or unrealistic expectations. Evaluate if your expectations are selfish, reasonable boundaries that have been violated by someone or rebellion in a passive or active manner.

Ô Sixth, forgive the person who "caused" your anger. The other person did not cause your anger, but it can feel that way. They just caused your expectation to not come to fruition. Forgive them; they revealed your expectations.

Ô Seventh, find and fix the common denominator in your anger. Repeated anger means unrealistic expectations. Unless you do something to find the expectation that is being trampled upon and fix or change, it you will continue to get angry.

Lust

It is always tragic when a great Christian leader is forced to the sidelines because of lust. We have all felt the pull of sexual desire that would draw us away from our goals and destroy our families. It must be resisted or your career, family, and reputation could lie in shambles. A number of years ago I was supposed to be interviewing a man for a pastoral job at a Denny's restaurant in our region. He was excited to be considered by one of our churches. He was, in fact, their leading candidate. After a lot of questions and interactions, I told him that I had heard something very disturbing about his ministry in his last church, and I just wanted to clear this up. I heard that he had been involved in an affair at the church. I looked him in the eye and asked, "Is it true?" He asked me where I had heard these things. I named a woman who had called me and told me that she had been in a long-term affair with him. I told him that she had called me when she heard that he was looking at taking another church. She and her counselor determined that she needed to speak out. The deep pain that gripped her life and marriage shouldn't be allowed to infect another family. He paused a long time before dropping his head and slowly answered, "Yes, it was true." He had seduced this prominent woman in the church during a rough patch in his own marriage. He had taken advantage of his position as pastor. His need for sexual passion almost destroyed this woman's marriage. It did destroy her husband's faith. It sent her into a deep depression that years later she is still not healed from. A few moments of stolen passion destroyed so much and now it was destroying his career in pastoral ministry.

I remember the great sadness that enveloped this man the next few times I met with him. His sexual desires had seduced him. He gave into lust's power and allowed this strong temptation to destroy his family, his reputation, and his career. He was stunned when he realized that eight years of college and seminary had been thrown away for a few moments of lust. What he had prepared to do all his life and what he was really good at were walled off and no longer available to him because he could not keep his pants on. DON'T LET THIS BE YOU.

What systems and routines need to be put in place to keep lust from winning?

Pick one of the exercises listed below and do it each day this week.

Let me suggest seven ways to keep sexual temptation from derailing your rise in leadership.

Ô　First, develop a growing dynamic loving marriage. Temptation is strongest when there is little sexual pleasure at home. Date, romance, and enjoy your spouse.

Ô　Second, personalize Roman 6:1-23. Write out the sixth chapter of Romans, inserting your name as often as you can and lust in the place of sin. This form of biblical meditation is a very strong deterrent to sexual temptation.

Ô　Third, clean up past sexual sins through confession. Sometimes a sexual temptation is particularly strong because it is a recurring temptation of what has been given into repeatedly earlier and not confessed. Confess what you have done individually and thoroughly and move in a different direction (1 John 1:9).

Ô　Fourth, eliminate all provisions for lust (Romans 13:14). Do not make lust convenient. Put accountability software on your computer. Remove adult channels from your TV service. Allow your spouse full access to your phone and appointment book.

Ô　Fifth, be on high alert when surrounded by lust's helpers: anonymity; convenience; loneliness; night; discouragement. (2 Timothy 2:22) It is much easier to give into the seduction of illicit sexual pleasure when you are anonymous, lonely, discouraged, and it is convenient. Be vigilant ahead of time for those times.

Ô　Sixth, get serious about resisting temptation; make it cost you something to give in (Hebrews 12:4). Get an accountability partner who can actually charge you money or take a toy away if you give in to lust.

Ô　Seventh, use the weapon of Scripture: The most powerful weapon in the leader's war with sin is the Word of God. Inject regular heavy doses into your soul. These are powerful verses for combating lust: Psalm 119:10-11; Romans 6:1-14; Galatians 5:16-23; 1 Thessalonians 4:1-9; Colossians 3:1-10.

Sloth: we call it procrastination now

In ancient times procrastination and poor time management were called sloth and laziness. It is that little impulse to put things off, to not put in the extra effort, to do just enough to get by, or to do what is convenient. Leaders fight against sloth in all its forms. How do you make sure that you do not give into procrastination? How do you manage your time effectively so that your life is balanced and ready to move forward at the right opportunity? How do you make sure that you do not become lazy?

There is also the opposite tendency in leaders which is to overwork, to become a workaholic. This is where the leader gets so many rewards from work that they neglect the other relationships of life. They are slothful about their marriage, about their family, and/or about their personal health while they keep pushing at work. There are always things to do.

What does it take to push back against procrastination and sloth? While this is a complex question, it usually boils down to our use of time. Every Christian leader must become self-disciplined with their time. Something inside of us is always pushing towards extremes: too much rest, too much work, excessive pursuit of pleasure. We must build systems and routines that allow us to work, rest, relate, enjoy, and love.

What systems and routines need to be put in place to keep sloth from winning?

Pick one of the exercises listed below and do it each day this week.

There are at least three key ideas that I have watched make all the difference for leaders.

Ô First, the pareto principle, which states that eighty percent of your results will come from only twenty percent of your activities. Therefore the leader must find the 20 percent productive activities and avoid the unproductive activities.

Ô Second, the planning principle, which states that every day, every week, every month, and every year key leadership actions must be inserted into one's schedule so that they will happen. Without planning those leadership actions will not happen, but status quo will reign.

Ô Third, the priority principle, which states that we all have ten relationships in our life that create a life worth living and each of them asks for too much time, too much energy, and too many resources. You can't give them all the same amount of time, energy, resources so these have to be rationed out by a biblical priority. Some people have allowed sloth to conquer vast territories in their life through the small convenient choice, the delay, or the continued work in the wrong direction. Do not allow sloth to steal your leadership or your life.

Gluttony

In ancient times gluttony was roughly equivalent to our modern day understanding of addictions. In those days there were only two major ways of self-medication to deal with problems, issues, and soul pain: food and drink. In our own day there are hundreds of different things which will dull the internal pain we don't want to deal with: alcohol, prescription drugs, illegal drugs, work, food, television, video games, pornography, promiscuity, violence, gambling, theft, etc. Addictions are a real danger and can derail almost any person's life and career. An addiction is a self-prescribed medication that dulls or eliminates an internal wound. If the wound is not dealt with, then continuing amounts of medication are needed until it is clearly done to excess.

Every Christian leader must avoid the trap of self-medication for their internal pain. Every Christian leader must process their pain, learn the lessons of their pain, and live in the real world full of broken, sinful people. This world is broken because of sin. All of us would like to retreat into a world where there is no pain, sorrow, or offenses; but that world is the one that is coming not the one we are living in. Gluttony is just a way of coping with the pain that this world dishes out. Be careful; there are so many ways to turn down a cul-de-sac and squander our one life.

What systems and routines need to be put in place to keep gluttony from winning?

Pick one of the exercises listed below and do it each day this week

Let me suggest four practical actions to keep gluttony from dominating your life.

Ô First, find a good counselor or trusted friend to tell your story and difficulties. We all need to process our pain with someone who will listen with intensity.

Ô Second, journal and pray your story to the Lord as your counselor. A good blank book which we fill with our thoughts and emotions can be one of the best counselors.

Ô Third, learn the lessons of the incident. Another way to work through the incidents of the past is to see how God may intend to use that experience to teach or construct something in your life. God is willing to use anything to develop the right qualities in our lives – the qualities of a blessed life. Ask yourself what qualities could be developed out of this difficult and painful aspect of your life.

Ô   Fourth, go to a support group for whatever issue you are facing. Many exist at churches and some are secular groups, but they do help as you battle against your self-medication tendency.

Greed

How much power does money have in your life? When was the last time you did something for free? How generous are you with the money you make? Does God get a portion of everything you make? When you see a person in need, are you tempted to help or do you move away from them? Is your feeling of success or satisfaction in life measured by your income or bank account? People are the most happy and fulfilled when they are doing what they were created to do, regardless of whether it makes them wealthy or not. Wealth promises fulfillment but never delivers. The lives of the wealthy are not filled with more fulfillment and satisfaction than the rest of the world. Instead, in many cases wealth has destroyed their lives. It has become a truism that the children and grandchildren of great wealth live wanton lives and have their purpose and incentives shredded by wealth.

Greed seeks to draw us off God's path into a world where all effort is evaluated by its monetary return. The seventh temptation to give into the dark side of leadership is greed. This means making all one's decisions based upon money or material gain. Great leadership decisions do not always go in this direction. Great leaders are trying to accomplish something greater than an increase of the bottom line.

Greed is what happens when you don't handle the power and pull of money well. The more gifted you are, the more opportunities for greed to creep into your life. Every Christian leader must develop systems to handle the love of money. Money promises more than it can deliver. It is not wrong to have money, but it is wrong to let it dominate you or to love it as though it can meet your needs.

Jesus says, "You cannot serve God and money." Each of us will have to choose. God has promised to take care of us if we would serve Him. It can be subtle but we can begin focusing on what we will receive rather than the job God has for us to do. The Apostle Paul says that the *love of money is the root of all sorts of evil.* (1 Timothy 6:13) The Apostle John speaks of the way to combat the work of greed in 1 John 2:15-18: *Do not love the world nor the things in the world. If anyone loves the world, the love of the Father is not in him. For all that is in the world, the lust of the flesh and the lust of the eyes and the boastful pride of life, is not from the Father, but is from the world.*

What systems and routines need to be put in place to keep greed from winning?

Pick one of the exercises listed below and do it each day this week?

> Let me suggest seven practical ways to battle against greed. Add bullet First, contentment. Reinvest in what God has already given you. Re-engage in your marriage. Enjoy your children or parents – whatever their ages or stages. Reconnect with old friends. There are joys to be discovered there.
> Ô Second, give ten percent of your income to the Lord's work as a rebuke to hoarding and stinginess. One of God's consistent antibiotics against greed is tithing a tenth of what you make to further God's work. It is not that God needs it as much as you need the practice of admitting that it all belongs to God.

Ô Third, become generous. Some people need to develop a generous lifestyle. This is giving beyond the tithe to people, causes, and organizations that really do alleviate human suffering, pain, and injustice.

Ô Fourth, begin doing some volunteer and charity work. When everything you do is compensated monetarily, then it is time to break out of that mold and volunteer. Don't let your life be reduced to an exchange of your time for someone else's money. Rebel and volunteer.

Ô Fifth, take a Sabbath each week to focus on God and rest. Do not use every day to make money. Do not keep pushing harder and faster. Realize that the only way to really recharge your spiritual and emotional batteries is by a long slow charge with God and others.

Conclusion

Most people have some kind of systems for pushing back the above dark desires. If not, everyone would descend into the depths of sin and depravity. However in many cases their systems don't work effectively, but they don't know what else to do so they stay with a broken routine hoping it will do a better job of protecting them from temptation the next time. It won't. They have not heard of God's systems or they have not been shown how to implement God's system in a way that is doable for them. They have not been trained in the implementation of God's system until it became second nature to them.

Great leadership requires not being pulled aside from the good that you could do by trivial, selfish, emotional, and impulsive pursuits. Each of us has been put on the earth for a purpose. The leader fulfilling their purpose positively affects the lives of dozens if not hundreds of people. There will be many times on the road to your destiny that you will have to say no to what you want to do.

It is worth it. Develop the above systems and barriers so that even when you want to sin, you won't or can't.

Leadership for a Change Exercises

At the end of each day, ask God to search your life and show you any ways that you gave into one of the seven deadly sins. If you did, then confess it and ask God to show you how to resist the next time.

At the end of each day, ask God to review your life and point out any way that you demonstrated any of the fruit of the spirit. Say each one of them and then pause and see if God brings to mind when and where you showed that quality.

CONCLUSION
LEADERSHIP FOR A CHANGE
Ten Essential Skills for Ministry Leadership

Darrel was called by God to lead a ministry. He threw himself into it and gave unselfishly of his time, energy, and resources. His ministry grew but it was completely wrapped up in what he did, was doing, or could do. His single-minded devotion to his ministry almost cost him his marriage and his devotional life with the Lord. We began to meet and talk about doing ministry through leadership rather than through personal charisma, energy, and time. He walked away from one ministry to heal his marriage. And a few years later he got involved in another ministry with his wife's full support. This time he began using his leadership gifts and skills. The ministry grew and grew and, at this writing, it is four times his previous ministry while he is putting in less than half the time. Ministry should not kill the messenger. Jesus said, "Come to me and I will give you rest. Take my yoke upon you and learn from me. And you will find rest for your souls." If your ministry is wearing you out, then you are probably not ministering through your leadership skills. Doing ministry can consume you, but leading ministry makes sure that you have an equal flow in and out.

When Pastor Darrell ministered out of his leadership skill set and gifts, he had time for his wife and children. He had time to pray and seek God's face about a balanced life. Don't try and do ministry without leadership skills or it will completely wear you out. I have had the privilege of helping train hundreds of leaders over the years. The programs that move a church forward change, but the need for leadership is constant. My hope is that you will practice the leadership skills in this book and lead your ministry better than you did before. We, the church of the living Christ, need you to be the best leader you can be.

Leadership is causing action in the right direction. Leadership has a set of skills to accomplish that movement in the right direction. We have talked about ten of the most essential skills of leadership, especially as it applies to ministry leadership. Leaders can become better at executing those skills. We can attract, hold, and direct more people in the right direction and have them less fatigued when they get there.

In this book we have drilled down into ten essential skills for ministry leadership. We have examined the need for leaders to grasp reality and not live in the fog of fuzzy results or best intentions. Ministry leaders cannot afford to pretend everything is fine if it is not. Too many ministries will have little or no results to hand over to Jesus because they have not been dealing with reality.

We have seen that leadership in ministry requires that we create and communicate a compelling vision. The right direction must be clear. We know that God's vision for ministry involves increased evangelism, discipleship, worship, compassion, and fellowship; but the specific dimensions and strategies will be varied from leader to leader. Ministry leaders must know where they are going and rally people to that future. A leader must get better and better at creating a clear and compelling image of the future. Unless the future already exists in our minds, then we won't be able to make it become real.

We have seen that leadership of a ministry requires that we become comfortable with initiating change and managing the change once it begins. There are ways to get a change started and unless a leader is willing to use them, nothing happens. Leaders must be practiced with those ways and willing to pull the trigger. Leaders must also grow in their ability to stay with and manage change as it is happening. The leader who starts change and walks away is less valuable than the one who makes sure that change is positive and not needlessly destructive. A ministry leader must become comfortable with the various aspects of the change process.

We have seen that being the leader of a ministry means that one knows how to work with people. It is not possible to lead well and treat people poorly. Ministry is a people business; therefore, leaders must be experts at attracting, encouraging, directing, and correcting people. Ministry is not producing widgets; it is producing better people, so ministry leaders must know the people business. Ministry leaders must forever be growing in their people skills.

We have seen that good ministry leaders know how to make wise decisions. Wisdom is in short supply in our world and it must show up in ministry decisions. Ministry leaders have learned how to collect wisdom and fight for the triple win: God must be glorified, people must win, and the leaders must win. Finding that nexus is not easy, but it is a part of what great ministry leading is about. Wisdom seldom comes in a rush but is a part of a process. Skilled leaders slow their decision making down to respecting the phases of a good decision in order to make sure they have the answers to the five crucial questions.

We have seen that leadership in ministry requires self-discipline or you will sabotage your own building success. Proverbs 13:6 tells us that iniquity subverts the way of those who get caught in it. Leadership is fraught with temptations, and they must be resisted if long-term positive change is to be achieved. Pride, Envy, Anger, Lust, Sloth, Gluttony, and Greed are listed as the seven deadly sins and they come to seduce the leader. Ministry leaders must watch their time, their emotions, and their personal weaknesses or they will squander their time as leaders.

We have seen that effective leadership of larger numbers of people requires sharing your systems and delegating to competent people. Leadership means trusting people and showing them the best ways to succeed. Great organizations are built on repeatable practical systems. It is not possible to lead many people well without a team, delegation, and clear procedures. Too many leaders try and become one-man shows and severely limit their effectiveness as leaders.

We have seen that leadership means recruiting the best people, next-level people for the ministry. The key number in every healthy ministry is how many leaders do you have in your ministry and is that number growing. Ministries go astray by putting too much on one or a few leaders. Ministries also go astray by hiring people who can take care of the present level of ministry instead of people who will create the next level of ministry. Ministry leaders who reach their maximal potential are constantly on the lookout for next-level leaders.

We have seen that ministry leaders must get over their fear of asking for funding for God's causes. It is not possible to accomplish great ministry goals without resources, and the leader must be center stage in that process. Ministry costs money, and it is up to the leaders to raise it. Ministry leaders must believe in the vision enough to ask people to give their money to make it happen. If the leaders do not believe in it that much, then it will not happen.

We have seen that leadership in ministry requires constant growth and development of leaders. Every current leader must be producing new leaders every year. If this isn't happening, then the ministry at best is stagnant. Every current leader must also be growing as a person and as a leader. They must feel that they are being developed, stretched, grown and cared for; not just used. And finally, the constant drains of ministry require that the key leader(s) make sure that they are replenished, growing, and developing.

Take a minute and look over the ten essential leadership skills for ministry and circle the two or three that you need to grow more skilled in using. Re-read those two or three chapters three separate times until the concepts and ideas are clear and actionable in your ministry. Take the actions that are outlined in those particular chapters. It is only when we act on information and practice skills that we truly grow and improve.

Ten Essential Ministry Leadership Skills
1. **Reality**
2. **Vision**
3. **People: Recruit Next-Level People**
4. **Leadership Development**
5. **Initiate and Manage Change**
6. **People**
7. **Wisdom**
8. **Systematize**
9. **Finances**
10. **Self-Discipline**

Please do not just read this book and then put it on the shelf with the other leadership books that you have read but not really applied. Change at least three things about your leadership because of this book. Improve in some way.

APPENDIX 1 - SAMPLE MINISTRY SYSTEMS

Assimilation system for following up visitors

- Ô Greeters in parking lot
- Ô Information table
- Ô Greeters at front door
- Ô Host and hostess
- Ô Gift in service
- Ô Pastor phone call
- Ô Gift drop by
- Ô Letter
- Ô Staff phone call
- Ô Specific info mailing
- Ô Newcomers Brunch invites
- Ô Newcomers Brunch

Five actions of a good greeter

- Ô Smile
- Ô Say "Hello"
- Ô Offer your name first
- Ô Extend your hand
- Ô Ask F.O.R. questions
  - Ò Family: Is this your family? Do you live around here?
  - Ò Occupation: What do you do for a living?
  - Ò Religion: How long have you been worshipping at Twin Lakes?

Seven actions of a good usher

- Ô Smile
- Ô Look people in the eye
- Ô Extend a bulletin
- Ô Say "Hello, welcome to Twin Lakes"

- Ô Offer to find them a seat: "May I find you a seat?"
- Ô Tell parents with small children that there is a nursery and offer to escort them
- Ô During the service, *immediately* approach a mother with a fussy baby and suggest that she go to the nursery

Seven actions of a good information booth worker

- Ô Smile
- Ô Look people in the eye
- Ô Say, "Hello, may I help you?"
- Ô Listen intently until the person finishes
- Ô Answer their question thoroughly
- Ô Ask them to fill out a guest card: "I would be happy to escort you to that location; would you please fill out this guest card first?"
- Ô Offer them coffee and/or donuts

Seven actions of a good runner

- Ô Smile
- Ô Look people in the eye
- Ô Say "Hello"
- Ô Offer your name first
- Ô Extend your hand
- Ô Take them *all* the way to place they are looking for
- Ô Walk *with* them pointing out where you going
- Ô Talk *positively* about the ministry they are going to

Church follow-up after the first visit

1. Pastor's letter
2. Visit
3. Volunteer phone call
4. Several cards
5. Staff phone call

6. Deacon or small group leader
7. Brunch or dessert gathering

Five actions of a good guest visit

Ô   Knock or ring the bell clearly
Ô   Smile
Ô   Say "Hello, we are from _____ Church. We just
     wanted to say thank you for stopping by our church today"
Ô   Hand them the gift. Do not stay more than five minutes
Ô   Say, "Thanks again" and turn to leave
Ô   If they are not home, leave the gift with a handwritten
     note that says, "Thanks for visiting with us at _____
     _____ Church"

Newcomers Brunch

Informal setting
Sharing why they started coming to the church
Hear from staff
Philosophy of the church:
Evangelism: We believe there are five important facts about
   heaven
Time to seek out staff of their interest
Food

Foundations Class: four weeks long

Small group of people – eight to twenty max
Sharing common info about each other
New life in Christ
Understanding the Bible
Understanding God
Understanding the Church

Prayer requests

Christian Maturity Class: six weeks long

Sharing common info about each other
Evangelistic presentation
Orthodoxy: three week brief overview of nine doctrines
Orthopraxy: three week brief overview of nine relationships
Take prayer requests; one per person
Close in prayer

Baptism Class: one week

Sharing common info about each other

Evangelistic presentation
Three New Testament pictures of baptism
Written declaration of surrender to Jesus Christ
Commitment of baptism
Baptism speech they will give (Personal Testimony)
The operational procedures of baptism

Membership Class

Sharing common info about each other
Evangelistic presentation and call
Declaration of surrender to Jesus and Church
Doctrine and constitution of this church
Philosophy of this church
Serving in this church; staff recruiters
Giving to this church

Small Group Meeting/Class

Open in prayer
Teach, show, or discuss the biblical content
Food
Take prayer requests
Close in prayer

Four keys of a good hospital visit

A Look: Make good eye contact with the person and ask them questions
A Word: Open the Bible read it and give them a word of encouragement
A Touch: Hold their hand or arm especially when you pray
A Prayer: Pray for them; listen what God would have you pray

Compassion Teams

Open in prayer: trust in God
Devotions from Team Leader: open the Bible
Doing Compassion: Loving people in the name of Jesus
Sharing experiences with a team of loving people
Sharing prayer requests
Invitation to the University of Life team
Closing in prayer

Developing men into godly leaders

Spiritual Disciplines: you must teach a man how to draw near to God on his own
Becoming a godly husband: men must know the basic skills of really loving their wife
Break free from lust to purity: men must know how to live free from lust
Time management: men must know how to prioritize their time to have a full life

Seven weekly actions of a great elder

- Ô Pray for the people of the church: divide the directory
- Ô Grow as a man of God
- Ô Minister in an area of the church
- Ô Give your wisdom not your opinion: Triple Win
- Ô Grow in each relationship of life: God, self, marriage, family, work, church, money, society, friends
- Ô Shepherd a small group: pray, Bible, witness, food, requests
- Ô Pray and work to see each system improve: Leadership – Equipping – Assimilation – Discipleship – Evangelism ÒResources – Spiritual – Heart – Organizational – Purpose

Seven weekly actions of a great deacon

- Ô Pray for the people, finances, and facilities of the church
- Ô Grow as a man of God: **Spiritual Disciplines**
- Ô Minister in an area of the church
- Ô Look for opportunities to physically and financially serve
- Ô Grow in each relationship of life: God, self, marriage, family, work, church, money, society, friends
- Ô Pray and work to see each system improve: finances – facilities

Seven weekly actions of a great pastor

- Ô Pray for the church and its people
- Ô Grow as a man of God: **Spiritual Disciplines**
- Ô Improve the eight areas: Children, Youth, Adult, Men's, Women's, Music, Facilities, Finances
- Ô Prepare and preach sermons that help real people
- Ô Grow yourself and others as leaders
- Ô Meet with the top twenty percent
- Ô Grow in each relationship of life: God, self, marriage, family, work, church, money, society, friends

Ô Pray and work to see each system improve: Leadership – Equipping – Assimilation – Discipleship – Evangelism ÒResources – Spiritual – Heart – Organizational – Purpose

Seven actions of a great worship leader

Ô Make eye contact with various people in the congregation
Ô Encourage: draw people into the presence of God
Ô Sing to God, not to impress others
Ô Lead with your voice: be strong, loud, and clear
Ô Eliminate pauses and silence between songs
Ô Point people to our great God
Ô Prepare yourself in spirit, soul, and body before Sunday to draw people into the presence of God

Seven actions of a great youth sponsor

Ô Pray for every young person and their family
Ô Grow as a man or woman of God: **Spiritual Disciplines**
Ô Look for opportunities to do ministry with youth & adults
Ô Prepare programs and teachings that really help students
Ô Meet, nurture, and care for a small group of youth
Ô Grow in each Relationship of Life: God, s elf, m arriage, family, work, church, money, society, friends
Ô Make sure that young people make positive growth each week

Seven weekly actions of a great youth pastor

Ô Pray for every young person and their family
Ô Grow as a man of God: **Spiritual Disciplines**
Ô Improve each youth system through prayer and hard work: Leadership – Equipping – Assimilation – Discipleship – Evangelism – Resources – Spiritual – Heart – Organizational ÒPurpose

- Ô Prepare programs and teachings that really help students
- Ô Grow yourself and others as leaders
- Ô Meet with the top twenty: leaders, influencers, potential leaders
- Ô Grow in each relationship of life: God, self, marriage, family, work, church, money, society, friends
- Ô Make sure that young people make positive growth each week

Seven actions of a great church member

- Ô Daily time of Bible study and prayer
- Ô Pray for the church, programs, and people
- Ô Give tithes and offerings from a willing heart
- Ô Look for opportunities to love Christians and non-Christians: meet needs, pursue people, please people
- Ô Serve in a ministry of the church
- Ô Participate in a Compassion Project: Ten Commandments; Prevention - Social Justice - Recovery
- Ô Do ministry whenever possible

Seven actions of a great prayer warrior

- Ô One to three hours of prayer per day
- Ô Listening hard to the Lord as to what to pray
- Ô Getting prayer lists from the pastor and the church
- Ô Praying the Scripture for individuals and churches
- Ô Recording your insights

Seven actions of a major ministry leader

- Ô Prayer
- Ô Biblical vision for the next six months
- Ô Connection with other major ministries
- Ô Recruiting people
- Ô Positive attitude

Ô Clarity about what is ministry
Ô Developing leaders: personal, skills, leadership

Seven actions of a great Sunday school teacher

Ô Daily time of Bible study and prayer
Ô Pray for the members of your class
Ô Evangelize the members of your class
Ô Prepare an interactive lesson for Sunday
Ô Write or phone the members of your class
Ô Reward those who bring a friend, their Bible, and an obedient spirit
Ô Attend church

Seven actions of a great Sunday school class

Ô Lots of talking, mingling, and caring for each other
Ô Warm greeting from the teacher
Ô Prayer to begin - prayer to close
Ô Engaging announcements about upcoming events
Ô Interactive lesson
Ô Age-appropriate applications from the Bible
Ô Life change commitments

APPENDIX 2 - SAMPLE ROUGH DRAFT VISION

The following is a general sample of the kind of document that might be produced for an imaginary church of five hundred.

Evangelism: We are believing God that one hundred fifty plus people will make professions of faith this next year through the ministries of the church. The following is a more detailed description of that vision:

> By this time next year, we believe that God wants this church to be doing these things in evangelism: three separate mass evangelism outreaches – one on Easter reaching one thousand people; one on Christmas Eve reaching twelve hundred people; one on Halloween reaching two thousand people; a clear presentation of the gospel to each person in the church each week; a visit to every new visitor to thank them for coming and to drop off a copy of the *Jesus* movie DVD; twenty neighborhood evangelistic discussion groups; three training classes on witnessing to neighbors, colleagues, and friends; support for fifteen missionaries from around the world; one missions emphasis week at the church to highlight the churches worldwide impact.

Discipleship: We are believing that three hundred plus people will be attending and growing in the various small groups during each of the three semesters that are offered at this church. A more detailed description of that general goal is:

> We believe that God wants us to pursue the following in discipleship: monthly church orientation classes – 101, 201, 301, 401; fifty sermon-based fellowship and

affinity groups; twenty-four content-based University of Life groups; fifteen ministry groups; ten leadership development action groups; four mission groups going outside of the country; fifteen trained lay counselors who can individually walk people through their life difficulties; fifty trained and equipped lay mentors who will work with people in the congregation for increased impact for Christ.

Worship and Celebration Arts: We believe that next year at this time fifty more people will be worshipping God and three new teams will be added to our celebration arts ministry. A more detailed breakdown of that vision is:

> We believe that God is calling us to strive and accomplish the following for his glory in worship and creative arts: fifty-two dynamic God-honoring, soul-stirring weekend services; four special choir opportunities; three performances at the local mall; once-a-month drama presentations; four children's worship dance performances; two photo and painting exhibits during the year; one church float in the Fourth of July parade.

Fellowship: We believe that God is going to add thirty new members and three new ways of being in relationship to this congregation. A detailed description of this idea is:

> We believe that God will have us honor Him by building community through the following ways: sixty percent participation of the Sunday morning attendance in some form of small group; a team of fifteen trained lay chaplains who will visit the sick in the hospital; meals provided for those undergoing surgery and/or having a baby; collecting a once-a-month supplemental

benevolent offering for the support of those in need in the congregation and community.

Service/Compassion: We believe that God wants every member of this church to be a minister serving at least two hours a week in the church and two hours a month in the community. A detailed look at these areas is:

We believe that God is calling our church to step outside of itself and present the love of Christ to our community and the world through compassion and social justice in the following ways: every small group will have one compassion/social justice project per quarter; the church will partner with the Salvation Army, the American Red Cross, the city of Woodland, and Compassion International to accomplish five separate compassion/ social justice actions this next year.

OTHER RESOURCES BY GIL STIEGLITZ

Books

Becoming Courageous
Breakfast with Solomon Volume 1
Breaking Satanic Bondage
Deep Happiness: The Eight Secrets
Developing a Christian Worldview
God's Radical Plan for Husbands
God's Radical Plan for Wives
Going Deep In Prayer: 40 Days of In-Depth Prayer
Leading a Thriving Ministry
Marital Intelligence
Mission Possible: Winning the Battle Over Temptation
Spiritual Disciplines of a C.H.R.I.S.T.I.A.N
They Laughed When I Wrote Another Book About
 Prayer, Then They Read It
Touching the Face of God: 40 Days of Adoring God
Weapons of Righteousness Study Guides
Why There Has to Be a Hell

**If you would be interested in having Gil Stieglitz
speak to your group, you can contact him
through the website
www.ptlb.com**